Queer Facts

The Greatest Gay & Lesbian Trivia Book Ever...

Printed and bound in Great Britain by MPG Books Ltd, Bodmin

Distributed in the US by Publishers Group West

Arcane is an imprint of Sanctuary Publishing Limited
Sanctuary House, 45–53 Sinclair Road
London W14 0NS, United Kingdom

www.sanctuarypublishing.com

Copyright © Michelle Baker, Stephen Tropiano, 2004

Cover: Dan Froude

ISBN: 1-86074-696-9

Queer Facts

The Greatest Gay & Lesbian Trivia Book Ever...

Michelle Baker & Stephen Tropiano

arcane

— FOREWORD —

This may not be true of everything in our lives, but at least when it comes to facts, gay men like them small. It seems we know the one big, important fact in our life – we like having sex – and everything else is simply unimportant, or trivial, if you will.

Heterosexuals get to talk about their wedding plans, their pregnancies, their children, their education and then their grandchildren. We, on the other hand, spend our time chatting about the new cologne from Michael Kors or some club's birthday bash on Saturday. Maybe it's also because we spend so much time talking to strangers; chatting about the weather doesn't really get you past foreplay, whereas a comprehensive list of companies that used gay-themed ads will get you all the way to the post-coital cigarette or perhaps even breakfast.

While all trivia interests us, we have of course a special fascination in facts and figures that relate to gay men and lesbians. I myself will be heading out to gay bars with an extra bit of conversational confidence now that I know which bisexuals, gay men and lesbians have appeared on US postage stamps. It is always a good thing to know when you are licking a gay head.

Obviously a great deal of what fascinates us is picked from popular culture, and so we want to know all about Melissa Etheridge or Martina Navratilova, but equally it is important to discover some of the smaller details from our gay and lesbian heritage, from the Roman author Lucian telling about butch and femme lesbians in AD160 to the buffet flats of Harlem in the late 1800s; it helps us to remember that we aren't the first generation to engage in *samlaingikta* (Hindi for *homosexuality*). Because we are all so open and, in general, accepted nowadays, it is easy to forget the thousands of years of secrecy, denial and special codes that went before. Although such little details of history come under the general heading of 'trivia', they are in fact very important to the gay and lesbian community. My fear is that, with all the tolerance we have achieved – the endless gay weddings, the huge proportion of gay and lesbian households that now have children – soon our conversation will become as dull and wholesome as those you hear at straight dinner parties.

I hope there never comes a time when I don't want to know that there are nearly 50 euphemisms for male masturbation involving food, because when that day arrives I'm guessing it means I've also lost interest in masturbation itself. Whether I'm buttering the corn, choking the chicken or tickling the taco, I know that I'll enjoy it more knowing that kings and queens have done it before me. It's oddly reassuring to find that gay men and lesbians have affected all sorts of realms, other than just the worlds of hairdressing and women's golf.

Leave this book on your coffee table and your only worry is that the trick you dragged home will become so engrossed by trivia that you won't ever get down to the most important pursuit of all. Bless Michelle and Stephen for slaving away at assembling this wonderful collection of facts and figures. In the long run, it's not going to change the world, but it will certainly make dinner conversation less dreary. Enjoy.

Graham Norton
October 2004

— PREDATORY DYKES —

Philosopher Denis Diderot's novel *La Religieuse* was published in France in 1796, after his death. In it, he includes a portrayal of a lusty Mother Superior who tries to seduce the young nun of the book's title. His characterisation of girl-for-girl attraction as emotionally depraved seemingly started a trend for 19th-century French novels. This representation was perpetuated by many 20th-century cinematic depictions of lesbianism and remains an entrenched stereotype today.

— LOVE OR THE CLOSET —

While many closeted movie stars were forced to enter into 'marriages of convenience' to create the illusion that they were heterosexuals, there was one who refused. William Haines gave up his career as a comic actor in silent films and early talkies when Louis B Mayer told him he had to get married, or else. Haines was released from his contract at MGM so that he could be with his lover, Jimmie Shields. Haines became a successful interior designer to the rich and famous and lived happily with Shields for 50 years until his death in 1973.

STUCK FOR WORDS? SOME HISTORICAL VARIATIONS — ON THE WORD 'BUTCH' —

There has been a host of terms used to refer to more masculine lesbians. In the mid 1900s, *sergeant* was popular, while in the 1930s *Apache* and *cat* were used. In the 1940s, as more women went out on the town courtesy of the liberty afforded by World War II, there was an abundance of terms such as *collar-and-tie*, *dandysette*, *shim*, *major*, *mantee* and *mason*. In the 1960s, there was the creative *pansy without a stem* and *jasper*, but by the 1970s there was the more literal *no-nuts*. In addition to these, there is also the following informative list:

brother-girl — bull dyke — big diesel — big diesel dyke
— bulldagger — diesel dyke — dagger — derrick —
Dutch girl — fellow — gal-officer — girl kisser —
goudou — goungnotte — grousse — he-she —
horsewoman — jota — king — king stud — lady-lover —
lasser — lesbo — many — penis-envy queen — polone
— poppa — pot — queer bird — queer queen —
sapphist — she-male — she-man — she-sexual

— THE GAY MAN'S HISTORY OF TELEVISION —

19 MARCH 1953   The first telecast of the Academy Awards live from the RKO Pantages Theater in Hollywood, hosted by Bob Hope.

31 MARCH 1957   Julie Andrews stars in a live telecast of Rodgers and Hammerstein's *Cinderella*. Kaye Ballard and Alice Ghostley co-star as her evil stepsisters.

28 APRIL 1965   Barbra Streisand's first TV special, *My Name Is Barbra*, premieres. She wins an Emmy for Outstanding Individual Achievement in Entertainment.

26 MARCH 1967   Mary Martin and Robert Preston host the first telecast of the Tony Awards from New York's Shubert Theater.

17 APRIL 1972   Bette Midler makes the first of 24 appearances on *The Tonight Show*, starring Johnny Carson. Twenty years later, she will be Mr Carson's final guest.

21 JUNE 1972   *The Corner Bar*, a sitcom set in a New York saloon, premieres on ABC. The short-lived comedy is the first to feature a gay series regular, designer Peter Panama, played by Vincent Schiavelli.

1 NOVEMBER 1972   *That Certain Summer*, the first made-for-TV movie about homosexuality, premieres. The story revolves around a teenager who finds out his father is gay.

13 APRIL 1983   *Dynasty*'s Krystal Carrington attacks Alexis Colby and the two slug it out in a lily pond.

5 JUNE 1983   Theatre producer John Glines accepts his Tony Award for Harvey Fierstein's *Torch Song Trilogy* and becomes the first gay man to thank his lover on national television. Harvey wins awards for Best Actor and Best Play.

21 DECEMBER 1983   *St Elsewhere* becomes the first dramatic series to devote a storyline to the AIDS crisis. One episode revolves around a married, closeted gay councilman diagnosed with the syndrome.

14 SEPTEMBER 1985   *The Golden Girls* debuts in the US.

11 NOVEMBER 1985   *An Early Frost*, the first made-for-TV movie about AIDS, premieres.

29 SEPTEMBER 1986   *Designing Women* begins its seven-year run.

12 NOVEMBER 1992   *Absolutely Fabulous* debuts in the UK. The sweetie-darlings over in America have to wait two more years before Patsy and Edina appear on Comedy Central.

23 JUNE 1994   The third season of MTV's *The Real World* debuts. The cast includes Cuban-born Pedro Zamora, a gay man living with AIDS.

30 APRIL 1997   In a historic episode of *Ellen*, Ellen DeGeneres and her TV alter-ego Ellen Morgan come out of the closet to 36.2 million viewers.

6 JUNE 1998   *Sex And The City* debuts in the US on Home Box Office.

21 SEPTEMBER 1998   *Will And Grace* (and Karen and Jack) debuts in the US.

23 FEBRUARY 1999   The original *Queer As Folk* debuts in the UK.

3 DECEMBER 2000   The premiere of the American version of *Queer As Folk* on Showtime.

— PUBLISHING TRIANGLE AWARDS —

The Publishing Triangle in the USA aims to further the publication of books and other materials written by lesbian and gay authors or with lesbian and gay themes. Founded in 1988, The Publishing Triangle and its affiliates present a number of awards each year, including:

- The Bill Whitehead Award for Lifetime Achievement

- The Judy Grahn Award for Lesbian Non-fiction

- The Randy Shilts Award for Gay Non-fiction

- The Audre Lorde Award for Lesbian Poetry

- The Triangle Award for Gay Poetry

- The Ferro-Grumley Award

- The Robert Chesley Award for Lesbian and Gay Playwriting

— WILDE MEN —

'Biography lends to death a new terror,' quipped Oscar Wilde, whose life has been dramatised extensively in feature films and on television. The following actors have had the honour of portraying the Irish poet, novelist, playwright and wit:

FEATURE FILMS
Robert Morley ....*Oscar Wilde* (1960)
Peter Finch..*The Trials of Oscar Wilde* (1960)
Nickolas Grace ....*Salome's Last Dance* (1988)
John DeMarco ....*The Best House in London* (1969)
Stephen Fry ....*Wilde* (1997)
Michael Culkin ....*An Ideal Husband* (1999)

TELEVISION
John O'Malley ....*Have Gun, Will Travel* (1958)
Richard Kneeland ....*Feasting with Panthers* (1974)
Peter Egan ....*Lillie* (1978)
Mark Eden...*Sorrell and Son* (1984)
Michael Gambon ....*Oscar* (1985)
Richard Strange ....*The Blackheath Poisonings* (1992)
Stephen Fry ....*Ned Blessing: The Story of My Life* (1993)

SOME COUNTRIES WHERE LESBIAN ACTS ARE — ILLEGAL —

Afghanistan	Algeria	Angola
Bahrain	Bangladesh	Barbados
Belize	Benin	Brunei
Cameroon	Cape Verde	Djibouti
Ethiopia	Grenada	Guinea (Conakry)
Iran	Lebanon	Liberia
Libya	Malawi	Mauritania
Morocco	Nicaragua	Oman
Pakistan	Puerto Rico	Qatar
Saint Lucia	Saudi Arabia	Senegal
Solomon Islands	Sudan	Swaziland
Syria	Togo	Trinidad and Tobago
Tunisia	United Arab Emirates	
Western Samoa	Yemen	

— THE FIRST LESBIAN PLAY ON BROADWAY —

On 29 September 1926, *The Captive*, a play about a young woman's seduction by an older woman, first appeared on Broadway.

— THE WIT OF TALLULAH BANKHEAD —

Tallulah Bankhead (1902–68) was a talented stage actress (*The Little Foxes* [1939], *The Skin Of Our Teeth* [1943]) who became best known in gay circles for her less-than-ladylike behaviour, her love affair with bourbon and her larger-than-life personality (she called everyone 'dahling'). Here are some of her best-known quotes:

- 'Cocaine isn't habit forming. I should know – I've been using it for years.'

- 'I am as pure as the driven slush.'

- 'I read Shakespeare and the Bible, and I can shoot dice. That's what I call a liberal education.'

- 'If I had to live my life again, I'd make the same mistakes, only sooner.'

- 'If you really want to help the American theatre, don't be an actress, dahling. Be an audience.

- 'It's one of the tragic ironies of the theatre that only one man in it can count on steady work: the night watchman.'

- 'It's the good girls who keep diaries; the bad girls never have the time.'

- 'Nobody can be exactly like me. Even I have trouble doing it.'

- On seeing a former lover for the first time in years: 'I thought I told you to wait in the car.'

— A STING IN THE TALE —

In Germany in 1919, Anna E Weirauch published the first of three volumes of her novel *The Scorpion*. It was one of the first widely read (and translated) books by a woman that featured lesbianism as its main theme.

— RIP: FINAL RESTING PLACES —

For those who wish to pay their respects to some esteemed ancestors, here's where you'll find them:

JAMES BALDWIN (1924–87), AMERICAN WRITER/CIVIL-RIGHTS ACTIVIST
Ferncliff Cemetery and Mausoleum, Hartsdale, New York

WILLIAM S BURROUGHS (1914–97), AMERICAN WRITER
Bellefontaine Cemetery, St Louis, Missouri

LORD GEORGE GORDON BYRON (1788–1824), ENGLISH POET
Hucknall Torkard Parish Church, Saint Mary Magdalen, Nottingham, England

JEAN COCTEAU (1889–1963), FRENCH FILM DIRECTOR/POET/PAINTER
Chapelle St Blaise, Milly La Forêt, Essone, France

JAMES DEAN (1931–55), AMERICAN ACTOR
Park Cemetery, Fairmount, Indiana

SERGEI MIKHAILOVICH EISENSTEIN (1898–1948), RUSSIAN FILM DIRECTOR
Novo-Devichy (Nowodjewchij), Moscow, Russian Federation

RAINER WERNER FASSBINDER (1946–82), FILM DIRECTOR
Bogenhausener Friedhof, Munich, Germany

PIER PAOLO PASOLINI (1922–75), FILM DIRECTOR
Cimitero di Casarsa, Friuli-Venezia Giulia, Italy

RUDOLPH VALENTINO (1895–1926), ACTOR
Hollywood Forever Cemetery, Hollywood, California

ANDY WARHOL (1928–87), ARTIST/FILMMAKER
St John the Baptist Byzantine Catholic Castle, Castle Shannon, Pennsylvania

OSCAR WILDE (1854-1900), DRAMATIST/NOVELIST
Cimetière du Père Lachaise, Paris, France

— LESBIAN CHAT —

That the internet has revolutionised the world will be news to no one. However, it's also had a radical impact upon the size of the lesbian (and gay) dating world. Ten years ago, few people would have considered a lonely-hearts advert as a means of meeting other, like-minded gals, yet today few lesbians are unaware of the dating potential offered by sites like www.gay.com and www.gaydargirls.com. These websites provide an opportunity to get to know someone via the written word, which is generally more helpful in building a solid basis for a relationship than 'Do you come here often?'.

A few words worth knowing if you're a lesbian 'newbie':

- Stats is your personal information: blk/bl = hair colour (black)/ eye colour (blue)

- ns = non-smoker

- LOL = laugh out loud (funny)

- LMLAO = laugh my lesbian arse off

- g/f = girlfriend

- str8 = straight

- ltr = long-term relationship

- f = femme, with its counterpart b(utch).

— CHILDREN IN US GAY AND LESBIAN HOUSEHOLDS –

One-third of US lesbian households and one-fifth of gay male US households have children.

— WHO WAS BILITIS? —

In 1894, Pierre Louÿs's novel *Les Chansons de Bilitis* was published, and in 1931 an uncensored version appeared, entitled *Les Chansons Secrètes de Bilitis*, which contained the explicit lesbian scenes that made it – and its author – famous. According to Louÿs, Bilitis was the daughter of a Greek and a Phoenician woman who left home to live on the island of Lesbos and there became part of Sappho's circle. While really just early heterosexual lesbian pornography, the name Bilitis was later used by Del Martin and Phyllis Lyon in their founding of the first lesbian political organisation in the USA, the Daughters of Bilitis.

— UK'S FIRST LESBIAN GROUP —

In London in 1963, five women founded the Minorities Research Group, the first lesbian organisation in the UK. Similar in intention to the American organisation Daughters of Bilitis, the group aimed to foster a community spirit amongst isolated lesbians. In 1965, some members later went on to found Kenric, a lesbian interest group that survives today.

BISEXUAL, GAY AND LESBIAN — NOBEL PRIZE WINNERS —

Vicente Aleixandre (1898–1984), Spanish poet..................*1977 Literature*
Jane Addams (1860–1935), American sociologist.....................*1931 Peace*
Bjørnstjerne Bjørnson (1832–1910), Norwegian
  playwright/novelist...1902 Literature
André Gide (1869–1971), French writer/critic..................*1947 Literature*
Dag Hammarskjöld (1905–61), Swedish Secretary General
  of the United Nations...*1961 Peace*
Selma Lagerlöf (1858–1940), Swedish writer.....................*1909 Literature*
Thomas Mann (1875–1955), German writer.....................*1929 Literature*
Roger Martin du Gard (1881–1958), French writer...........*1937 Literature*
Patrick White (1912–90), Australian writer.......................*1973 Literature*
Jacinto Benavente (1866–1954), Spanish writer.................*1922 Literature*

— 'YEP, I'M GAY' —

Bisexual/gay men who have played themselves in movies:

William S Burroughs in *Prologue* (Canada, 1970)

Quentin Crisp in *To Wong Foo, Thanks For Everything! Julie Newmar* (US, 1995)

Rainer Werner Fassbinder, *Germany In Autumn* (West Germany, 1978)

Jean Genet in *Prologue* (Canada, 1970)

André Gide in *La Vie Commence Demain (Life Begins Tomorrow)* (France, 1952)

Allen Ginsberg in *Prologue* (Canada, 1970) and *Ciao! Manhattan* (US, 1972)

David Hockney in *A Bigger Splash* (UK, 1974)

Sir Elton John, *The Ryan White Story* (US, TV-M, 1989)

Sir Ian McKellen in *Thin Ice* (UK, 1995)

Stephen Sondheim in *Camp* (US, 2003)

— 'DON'T GIVE THEM IDEAS!' —

At no time has sex between women been a criminal offence in the UK. However, in the summer of 1921, the British House of Commons decided that there were enough suspected shenanigans to justify changing this. They voted 148 votes to 53 under the Criminal Law Amendment Bill to criminalise lesbian activity and behaviour in the same way as that of male homosexuals. The Bill was subsequently sent to the House of Lords, where it was rejected on the basis that it would merely draw attention to lesbianism and might invoke in women thoughts that they would never previously have entertained, about matters that they might not understand!

— AUSSIE (MILITARY) RULES —

On 23 November 1992, Australia's Prime Minister, Paul Keating, revoked the country's restrictions on gay men and lesbians in the military.

— 'HOMOSEXUALITY' IN ANCIENT GREECE —

Labels such as 'heterosexual', 'bisexual' and 'homosexual' didn't exist in ancient Greece. Sexual relations were defined in terms of the role one assumed in the sexual act, which was in accordance with the political structure of the state.

In Athens (*circa* fifth century BC), an adult male citizen assumed the 'active' role in sex with anyone who was inferior in social and political status – namely women, girls, boys, foreigners and slaves.

Pederasty (adult men loving boys) and philerasty (boys loving adult men) were institutionalised sexual practices between an adult male (the *erastes*, derived from *eran*, meaning 'lover') and a boy (the *eromenos*, derived from the Greek god Eros, a winged youth who makes a person fall in love with or desire another individual). The *erastes* typically met his *eromenos* at the gymnasium, which was the social centre of Athenian life.

The origin of the *erastes–eromenos* relationship has been traced back to prehistoric Crete. According to first-century BC writer Strabo of Amaseia, homosexual relations were part of an initiation ritual involving the pre-arranged kidnapping of young city boys by older men, who took the lads away from the city for months of hunting, feasting and homosexual sex. After the initiation was completed, each boy received a military outfit, an ox to sacrifice to Zeus and a drinking cup for wine.

While sexual relationships between a man and a male youth were acceptable in ancient Greece, sexual relations between two adult male citizens were forbidden. The Greeks believed that the patriarchal power structure of the State would be undermined if an adult male assumed the passive position in sexual relations with another man.

Homo-erotic relationships in Greek mythology mirror the *erastes–eromenos* paradigm: Zeus falls for young Ganymede, who is kidnapped and transported to Mount Olympia to be the god's wine-pourer; Poseidon does the same to young Pelops; and Laius, the mythical founder of *paiderasteia* (the institution of pederasty), falls for young Chrysippus.

— AMAZONS —

The concept of the Amazon comes from Greek mythology, which makes references to a race of female warriors. These tales gave rise to legends that shared similar features, such as:

- The women came from the east;

- They founded a society of women in northeast Asia Minor;

- They worshipped Ares and Artemis.

There the commonalities in legends end and differing (sometimes conflicting) details emerge. These include the notion that, for preservation of the race, Amazons socialise for sexual purposes for two months of the year, and only female children are kept. There is also the (probably false) belief that the Amazon would cut off one breast so that she could shoot her bow and arrow more accurately, which is possibly based on the erroneous etymological assumption that the word *Amazon* comes from *a* (meaning 'without') and *mazos* (meaning 'breast'), although historical depictions all show them to be intact! Whatever their origin and history – or even if the Amazons actually existed – lesbians and heterosexuals have both long been intrigued by the possibility that such a race of women could exist. The Amazon is an appealing and enduring representation of women who can exist without men.

— L'AMAZONE —

'L'Amazone' was the nickname by which early-20th-century Parisians knew the lesbian patron of the arts Natalie Barney (1876–1972), an outspoken woman with right-wing sympathies atypical of Modernist lesbians of the period.

Barney ran one of the two major artistic salons of that time, the other being run by Gertrude Stein. The Salon, at 20 rue Jacob, was thoroughly apolitical and provided patronage for lesbian and gay artists; L'Amazone herself was a poet, and writers such as Radclyffe Hall, Djuna Barnes, Marcel Proust and André Gide were part of her entourage. The American painter Romaine Brooks and poet Renée Vivien were additional visitors and purportedly also her lovers.

As the Pullman-car heiress, Barney was incredibly wealthy and is said to have been uninterested in developing feminist politics that extended beyond class and culture. She was openly lesbian in her poetry and wrote a collection of thoughts about homosexuality entitled *Pensées d'une Amazone*.

— CAMP STAMPS —

A rundown of bisexual, gay men, and lesbians who appear on US postage stamps:

Jane Addams, social reformer
Leonard Bernstein, composer
Willa Cather, writer
Stephen Foster, composer
Cole Porter, composer
Lorenz Hart, lyricist
Margaret Mead, anthropologist
Bessie Smith, singer
Rudolph Valentino, actor
Andy Warhol, artist
Tennessee Williams, writer

— GRETA GARBO, BISEXUAL RECLUSE —

Born in 1905, the Swedish actress Greta Garbo is renowned as having been one of the most enigmatic and secretive of all Hollywood's stars. One of her most famous lines to the press, 'I want to be let alone', is usually misquoted as 'I want to be alone'. Her portrayal of masculine roles in masculine attire has led to an enduring reputation as a queer icon, and both men and women revere her. Her most famous lesbian role was her portrayal of Queen Christina, with which she has garnered for herself a place in the annals of lesbian history forever; and it is said that her lesbian-coded portrayal of the monarch was based on the actress's much-speculated -about affair with scriptwriter Mercedes de Acosta. A recluse since her retirement in 1941, she died in 1990.

— OSCAR AND WALT —

While on his 1882 lecture tour across the US, Irish poet and playwright Oscar Wilde paid a visit to fellow poet Walt Whitman. Whitman later described Wilde as 'the grandest man I have ever seen'. After a second meeting, Wilde confided to a friend, 'The kiss of Walt Whitman is still on my lips.'

— IF THEY WEREN'T GAY ENOUGH ALREADY! —
GAY-POPULAR MOVIES TURNED INTO BROADWAY MUSICALS

Movie	Musical	Number Of Performances	Tony winner Best Musical?
All About Eve (1950)	Applause (1970–72)	896	√
42nd Street (1933)	42nd Street (1980–89)	3,486	√
Footloose (1984)	Footloose (1998)	709	
Grand Hotel (1932)	Grand Hotel (1989–92)	1,018	
La Cage Aux Folles (1978)	La Cage Aux Folles (1983–87)	1,761	√
The Producers (1968)	The Producers (2001–)	1,334+	√
Saturday Night Fever (1977)	Saturday Night Fever (1999–2000)	501	
Some Like It Hot (1959)	Sugar (1973)	505	
Sunset Boulevard (1950)	Sunset Boulevard (1994–97)	977	√
Thoroughly Modern Millie (1967)	Thoroughly Modern Millie (2002–04)	919	√
Victor/Victoria (1982)	Victor/Victoria (1995–97)	734	
The Wizard Of Oz (1939)	The Wiz (1975–79)	1,672	√

— FIRST US GAY OR LESBIAN POLITICIAN —
ELECTED TO A STATE OFFICE

On 5 November 1974, Elaine Noble became the first openly lesbian or gay politician to be elected to a US state office when a Boston district voted her in as its representative to the Massachusetts legislature.

— MELISSA ETHERIDGE: FACTS YOU SHOULD KNOW —

BIRTHDAY: 29 May 1961

STUDIED AT: Boston's Berkely College of Music

DEBUT ALBUM: *Melissa Etheridge* (May 1988, Island Records)

BIGGEST SINGLE: 'I'm The Only One' (1994)

THREE TOP TEN HITS: 'Come To My Window'
'I'm The Only One'
'If I Wanted To'

BIGGEST LP: *Yes I Am* (September 1993)

GRAMMY AWARDS: Two

CAME OUT: 1992, presidential inauguration of Bill Clinton

CHILDREN: Two – Bailey Jean (daughter, born February 1997) and Beckett (son, born November 1998), both with former partner Julie Cypher (together from 1988–2000) and with the collaboration of David Crosby.

MARITAL STATUS: Married, to Tammy Lynn Michaels, in September 2003

— ACROSS THE FRUITED PLAIN —

A selection of 'gay' (in name only) American communities:

Gay Creek, Alaska
Gay Creek, California
Gay Mountain, California
Gay, Georgia
Gayway Corner, Idaho
Gays, Illinois
Gaylord, Kansas
Gays Creek, Kentucky
Gay Brook, Maine
Gay Cove, Maine

Gay Hill, Maine
Gay Island, Maine
Gay Head, Massachusetts
Gay, Michigan
Gay, Mississippi
Gay Lemon Park, Mississippi
Gays Branch, Mississippi
Gay Creek, Montana
Gay Lake, Nevada
Gay Brook, New Hampshire
Gaylord Peak, New Mexico
Gayhead, New York
Gayville, New York
Gay, North Carolina
Gaylord, North Dakota
Gaysport, Ohio
Gay, Oklahoma
Gaylord, Oregon
Gaysport, Pennsylvania
Gay Oaks, South Carolina
Gay Hill, Texas
Gay, West Virginia
Gays Mills, Wisconsin

— AHOY, ME LAND LOVERS —

Anne Bonney (1697–?) was the most notorious pirate of the 18th century. The daughter of a wealthy lawyer and a tomboy in her early years, she was disinherited by her father, reportedly for 'disgraceful behaviour'. In reaction, she set fire to the family plantation and subsequently fled to the port of New Providence. She then sailed the high seas with her companion, Mary Read, who was given her dead brother's name, Mark, as a child and was dressed as a boy by her mother to secure an inheritance. Reports indicate that they were physically intimate and remained inseparable despite their various marriages to men. Both pirates were caught and tried for piracy in 1720 but escaped hanging by pleading pregnancy. Documentation exists that describes Mary's death of an illness in jail, but no further records pertaining to Anne exist. The notorious pirate was so famous that, in America in 1951, director Jacques Tourneur filmed a fictionalised portrait of her life, titled *Anne Of The Indies*.

GAY, LESBIAN, AND BISEXUAL
— PULITZER PRIZE WINNERS —

BIOGRAPHY

A Scott Berg	1999	*Lindbergh*

DRAMA

Zoe Akins	1935	*The Old Maid*
Edward Albee	1975	*Seascape*
	1967	*A Delicate Balance*
	1994	*Three Tall Women*
Michael Bennett	1976	*A Chorus Line*
Michael Cristofer	1977	*The Shadow Box*
Nilo Cruz	2003	*Anna In The Tropics*
Nicholas Dante	1976	*A Chorus Line*
Margaret Edson	1999	*Wit*
William Inge	1953	*Picnic*
James Kirkwood	1976	*A Chorus Line*
Tony Kushner	1993	*Angels In America*
John Patrick	1954	*Teahouse Of The August Moon*
Stephen Sondheim	1985	*Sunday In The Park With George*
Paula Vogel	1998	*How I Learned To Drive*
Thornton Wilder	1938	*Our Town*
	1943	*The Skin Of Our Teeth*
Tennessee Williams	1948	*A Streetcar Named Desire*
	1955	*Cat On A Hot Tin Roof*
Lanford Wilson	1980	*Talley's Folly*
Doug Wright	2004	*I Am My Own Wife*

FICTION

Willa Cather	1923	*One Of Ours*
John Cheever	1979	*The Stories Of John Cheever*
Alice Walker	1983	*The Color Purple*
Thornton Wilder	1928	*The Bridge Of San Luis Rey*

MUSIC

Samuel Barber	1958	*Vanessa*
	1963	*Piano Concerto No. 1*
Aaron Copland	1945	*Appalachian Spring*
John Corigliano	2001	*Symphony No. 2 For String Orchestra*
David Del Tredici	1980	*In Memory Of A Summer Day*

Gian-Carlo Menotti	1950	*Music In The Consul*
	1955	*The Saint Of Bleecker Street*
Ned Rorem	1976	*Air Music*
Virgil Thompson	1949	*Music For The Film* Louisiana Story

POETRY

John Ashberry	1976	*Self-Portrait In A Convex Mirror*
WH Auden	1948	*The Age Of Anxiety*
Elizabeth Bishop	1956	*Poems – North And South*
Richard Howard	1970	*Untitled Subjects*
Amy Lowell	1926	*What's O'Clock*
William Meredith	1988	*Partial Accounts: New And Selected Poems*
James Merrill	1977	*Divine Comedies*
Edna St Vincent Millay	1923	*The Ballad Of The Harp-Weaver And Other Poems*
Marianne Moore	1952	*Collected Poems*
James Schuyler	1981	*The Morning Of The Poem*

— HOWDY, PARDNER! —

An old cowboy dressed in cowboy shirt, hat, jeans, spurs and chaps goes to a bar, sits down and orders a drink. As he is sipping his whiskey, a woman sits down next to him. She orders her drink, turns to the cowboy and asks 'Are you a real cowboy?'.

He replies, 'Well ma'am, I've spent my whole life on the ranch, herding cows, breaking horses and mending fences, so I guess I am.'

After a short while, he asks what she is. She replies, 'I've never been on a ranch, so I'm not a cowboy, but I am a lesbian. I spend my whole day thinking about women. As soon as I get up in the morning, I think of women. When I eat, shower, watch TV, everything seems to make me think of women.'

A short while later she leaves and the cowboy orders another drink. A couple sit down next to him and ask 'Are you a real cowboy?' To which he replies, 'Well, I always thought I was, but I just found out I'm a lesbian.'

— WHO WAS SAPPHO? —

Sappho was an early Greek poet who founded a school for girls on the island of Lesbos (aka Lesvos). She was one of the earliest writers of lyric poetry, but today most of her poems are preserved only as fragments. Her poetry contains abundant references to women loving other women, and her all-female island gave the name to an entire way of being nearly 2,000 years after its heyday. Sappho is said to have lived from about 620BC to 560BC and her poetry was highly regarded by her peers, to the extent that Plato called her the Tenth Muse. Her legacy to the world was to give a name to an entire race of women who loved women in a sexual way; the term *sapphist* was in use in France and England in the 18th century to infer lesbian. While the term isn't in common use today, most people know that Sappho was a right-on lesbian.

— LEYENDECKER AND THE ARROW COLLAR MAN —

Joseph C Leyendecker (1874–1951) was one of America's leading commercial artists (second only to Norman Rockwell) who became best known for creating the advertisements for Arrow collars and shirts. The handsome model wearing an Arrow shirt in the ads epitomised the masculinity and sophistication of the American male. What the public didn't know is that the model was actually Leyendecker's lover, Charles Beach (1886–1952). The artist and his model were together for 49 years until Leyendecker's death in 1951.

— IT'S JUST A LITTLE CRUSH —

By the late 19th and early 20th century, women were spending much more time together in educational institutions. This led to the growth of the so-called Romantic Friendship, but also to another youthful phenomenon amongst girls: the adolescent crush on girls in your circle. It became so common that it had a vernacular of its own, and slang words for the infatuation abounded, including...

Crush – Rave – Spoon – Pash (passion) –
Smash – Gonage ('gone on') – Flame

— THE ORIGIN OF SODOMY LAWS —

The term 'sodomy' originates from the biblical story of the ancient cities of Sodom and Gomorrah, which were destroyed by God for their sin and depravity. In Genesis 19:4–9, two angels are sent by God to deliver Lot and his family safely away from the city. Lot sheltered the two angels in his house, which is soon surrounded by the city's male citizens, who want to 'know' (ie rape) the male angels. Lot protects the angels by offering the mob his two virginal daughters. The angels' subsequent destruction of the city by fire and brimstone has been interpreted as a condemnation of homosexuality and cited as the 'divine source' of anti-sodomy laws.

In addition to the Sodom and Gomorrah story, two passages from the book of Leviticus, written in the fifth century BC, are the Judeo-Christian sources for anti-sodomy laws:

- 'Thou shalt not lie with mankind as with womankind; it is abomination.' (Leviticus 18:22)

- 'And if a man lies with mankind, as with womankind, both of them have committed an abomination; they shall surely be put to death; their blood shall be upon them.' (Leviticus 20:13)

In both the United States and western Europe, Leviticus 18:22 and 20:13 were incorporated into early sodomy laws.

As a legal term, 'sodomy' encompasses a wide range of sexual acts, including fellatio, masturbation and bestiality. The primary function of early sodomy laws was to persecute adult males who engaged in sexual relations with other adult males, young boys or animals. In accordance with biblical writings, convicted adult male sodomites were condemned to death by decapitation, hanging or burning at the stake.

— EARLIEST BUTCH-FEMME RELATIONSHIP — IN LITERATURE

In about AD160, the Roman author Lucian gave us an insight into the lives of the *tribades* of Rome. In the fifth of his *Dialogues Of The Courtesans*, one particular courtesan tells the tale of how she was seduced by a wealthy female couple who had what is probably the earliest example of a butch-femme relationship.

— TRUMAN CAPOTE'S BLACK-AND-WHITE BALL —

Considered by many as the social event of the century, in 1966 Truman Capote hosted a black-and-white ball in honour of his good friend, publisher and Washington, DC socialite Katharine Graham. Capote asked the men to wear dinner jackets with black masks, while the women wore black or white dresses with white masks. Guests sipped Tattinger champagne and danced to the sounds of Eddie Duchin and his orchestra. The supper, served at midnight, included chicken hash with sherry, spaghetti bolognese, pastries and coffee. Total cost: $13,000.

The 540 names on the guest list included:

Edward Albee
Lauren Bacall
James Baldwin
Tallulah Bankhead
Cecil Beaton
Marisa Berenson
William F Buckley
Claudette Colbert
Sammy Davis, Jr
Mrs Henry Ford
Arlene Francis
Henry J Heinz
Christopher Isherwood
Rose Kennedy
Bobby Kennedy
Ted Kennedy
Jacqueline Kennedy
Alice Roosevelt Longworth
Mr and Mrs Norman Mailer
Marianne Moore
William and Babe Paley
Jerome Robbins
Arthur Schlesinger, Jr
Mia Farrow and Frank Sinatra
Lionel and Diane Trilling
Andy Warhol
Robert Penn Warren
Duke and Duchess of Windsor

THE MARVEL OF MARTINA:
— WHAT YOU MAY NOT KNOW —

The most successful player of either gender in tennis history, Martina Navratilova was born on 18 October 1956 in Prague, Czechoslovakia. After her parents separated, she moved with her mother to Revnice, which was the birthplace of her interest in tennis. Her mother remarried in 1962 and her stepfather, Mirek Navratil, became her first coach.

- Played in her first junior tournament in 1964 and became a professional player in 1973, reaching the quarter-finals of her first Grand Slam event.

- Became a US resident in September 1975, finally becoming a citizen on 21 July 1981.

- Played on the WTA Tour, competing in the singles from 1973 until the present day, with her 2004 Wimbledon wildcard entry at the age of 47.

- Won 18 major singles titles from 1978 to 1990, including nine at Wimbledon.

- Represented the USA for the first time at the 2004 Olympics.

- Won 167 singles titles and 173 doubles titles.

- Personal trainer is Gisella Tirado, a successful Australian touch player.

- Enjoys snow skiing, snowboarding, golf, basketball and horseriding.

- Released an autobiography, *Martina*, in 1985.

- Co-wrote three mystery novels: *The Total Zone* (1995), *Breaking Point* (1996) and *Killer Instinct* (1998).

- Participated in the creation of Rainbow Cards, a credit card aimed at the gay and lesbian population.

- Constant companion is her chihuahua, Chloe.

- Inducted into the International Tennis Hall of Fame in Newport, Rhode Island, USA, in 2000.

— ORIGIN OF THE WORD 'DYKE' —

Much has been speculated about the origin of the word *dyke* (sometimes *dike*). Recorded as far back as 1851, the word then referred to a man dressed formally for social occasions and who was said to be 'diked out'. By 1900, the word *bulldyker* had come to be used in the red-light district of Philadelphia to mean lesbian lovers. Later, by 1935, black blues singer Bessie Jackson had recorded a song titled 'B-D Woman', meaning 'Bulldagger Woman', which went on, in a knowing manner, about women who adopted a masculine style. Originally the term was abusive but was reclaimed by 1970s lesbians and is still used today by the female gay community as a positive term, despite many heterosexuals (and some lesbians) still finding offence in the term.

— HOMO 101 —

ONE, Inc, was one of the earliest gay-rights organisations in the US, founded in the 1950s. In an effort to educate the public about the subject of homosexuality, the group opened the ONE Institute, which offered courses on a variety of homo-themed subjects. Here is a sampling of course titles from the Institute's early catalogues:

An Introduction to Homophile Studies (November 1956)
Homosexuality in History (fall 1957/spring 1958)
A Symposium: How Homosexuality Fits In (November 1957)
Homosexuality: A Way of Life (midwinter 1958)
Mental Health and Homosexuality (midwinter 1959)
Homosexuality in Modern German History (1959–60)
Landmarks in Homophile Literature (1959–60)
The Homosexual and the Community (midwinter 1960)
The Orthodox Freudian Texts on Homosexuality (spring 1960)

— KIKI —

When butch-and-femme was the *de facto* rule in the bars, this was a derogatory term for someone who was neither.

— STRAIGHT, YET GAY —

A list of 'gay-acting' heterosexual TV characters:

CHARACTER	ACTOR	SHOW
Uncle Arthur	Paul Lynde	*Bewitched*
Felix Unger	Tony Randall	*The Odd Couple*
Niles, the Butler	Daniel Davis	*The Nanny*
Chandler Bing	Matthew Perry	*Friends*
Maj Charles Winchester	David Ogden Stiers	*M*A*S*H*
Nigel Wick	Craig Ferguson	*The Drew Carey Show*
Dr Frasier Crane	Kelsey Grammer	*Frasier*
Dr Niles Crane	David Hyde Pierce	*Frasier*
Harrison Otis Carter	Gale Gordon	*Here's Lucy*
Dr Zachary Smith	Jonathan Harris	*Lost in Space*
Detective Ron Harris	Ron Glass	*Barney Miller*
Arnold Horschack	Ron Palillo	*Welcome Back, Kotter*
Mel Cooley	Richard Deacon	*The Dick Van Dyke Show*
Mr Robinson Peepers	Wally Cox	*Mr Peepers*
Henry Warnimont	George Gaynes	*Punky Brewster*
Claymore Gregg	Charles Nelson Reilly	*The Ghost and Mrs Muir*
Andrew J Lansing	Paul Reubens	*Murphy Brown*
Mr Harry Bentley	Paul Benedict	*The Jeffersons*
Monroe Ficus	JM J Bullock	*Too Close For Comfort*

— GLOBAL CHICK CHAT —

To meet other lesbians on line, try one of the following websites:

www.gay.com
www.girlbar.com/lesbiannetwork.html
www.girldates.com
www.lesbianation.com
www.technodyke.com
www.gaydargirls.com

— FIRST ORDAINED LESBIAN US RELIGIOUS LEADER —

On 10 January 1977, the Episcopal Church ordained Ellen Marie Barrett, making her the first openly lesbian cleric of any major religious organisation in the US.

— LESBIAN AND LESBIAN/GAY PUBLICATIONS —

Title	Era	Country Of Origin	What It's About
Albatross	1970s	America	Satirical magazine
Black/Out	founded 1986	America	Biannual magazine for lesbian and gay men of colour
BLK	founded 1988	America	Monthly magazine for black lesbians and gay men
Camp Ink	1970	Australia	First ever Australian gay magazine, produced in Sydney by CAMP
Campaign	1975+	Australia	Monthly gay magazine
Chana con Chana	founded 1982	Brazil	Brazilian lesbian magazine. English translation means 'cunt to cunt'
Conditions	founded 1976	New York	Feminist journal with an emphasis on new writing by lesbians, concentrating on issues of race and class in lesbian action
Diva	founded 1994	UK	Best-selling dyke mag in Europe
Dykes, Disabilities And Stuff	USA		Quarterly magazine for lesbians and feminists with disabilities. Carries news, features, letters to the editor, reviews, fiction, poetry and drawings
The Freewoman	early 20th C	England	Although not explicitly lesbian (in keeping with the feminist movement of the time that would not be seen to be promoting lesbian rights), this publication was the only feminist organ to discuss issues of same-sex eroticism

Title	Era	Country Of Origin	What It's About
The Furies	1972	USA	Lesbian-feminist monthly
The Ladder	1956	USA	Monthly publication of Daughters of Bilitis and probably the first widespread lesbian publication
LOTL	1989	Australia	Informative, concise publication with a predominantly contemporary perspective
On Our Backs	1984	USA	Lesbian sex mag that encourages sexual exploration and empowerment

— HOMOPHOBIA 101: —
WHAT'S WRONG WITH THOSE PEOPLE?

The word *homophobia* was coined by heterosexual clinical psychologist George Weinberg in his 1971 treatise *Society And The Healthy Homosexual*. Weinberg was a member of the Gay Activists Alliance, one of the early gay and lesbian civil-rights groups, formed a few months after the Stonewall Riots of December 1969.

In a 2002 interview with gaytoday.com, Weinberg recalled the moment in 1965 when the word came to him: 'I remember the moment in 1965 when it came to me with utter clarity, that this was a phobia. I was preparing a speech for a homophile group, which set me to thinking about "What's wrong with those people?"' By 'those people', Weinberg is referring to a few therapist friends who spoke well about a female friend of his until he told them that she was a lesbian.

'The roots of homophobia are fear, fear and more fear,' Weinberg explains. 'It is based on the preposterous notion that if you are like everybody else you will be safe, secure and happy. And, in the extreme, that if you are good, you won't die. "Well, no wonder he died, he smoked a few joints." Or "He went to India." Or "He was homosexual. I would never do that."'

— SPORTS DYKES —

Lesbians have often found companionship and partners upon the sportsfield.
Here are a few professional athletes who've been sufficiently comfortable
with their sexuality to be sporty-dykes. Some, however, did not come out
of their own volition but were outed.

SPORTY-DYKE	COUNTRY	SPORT
Jenny Allard	USA	Softball
Camilla Andersen	Denmark	Handball
Mia Hundvin (Andersen's ex)	Norway	Handball
Alyson Annan	Australia	Field hockey
Carol Thate (Annan's partner)	The Netherlands	Field hockey
Betty Baxter	Canada	National volleyball coach
Carol Blazejowski	USA	Basketball
Carin Clonda	Australia	Squash
Conchita Martinez	Spain	Tennis
Nancy Drolet	Canada	Ice hockey
Missy Giove	USA	Mountain biking
Ramona Gatto	USA	Kickboxing
Pat Griffin	USA	Coach, author, educator
Gina Guidi	USA	Boxing
Savoy Howe	Canada	Boxing
Helen Hull Jacobs	USA	Tennis
Billie Jean King	USA	Tennis
Nicole LaViolette	Canada	Cycling
Amelie Mauresmo	France	Tennis
Jen Moore	USA	Softball
Martina Navratilova	USA	Tennis
Diana Nyad	USA	Long-distance swimming
Andrea Ratkovic	USA	Duathalon
Lauren Ruffin	USA	Basketball
Patty Sheehan	USA	Golf

SPORTY-DYKE	COUNTRY	SPORT
Lisa-Marie Vizaniari	Australia	Discus
Muffin Spencer-Devlin	USA	Golf
Karrie Webb	Australia	Golf
Sue Wicks	USA	Basketball
Aylssa Wykes	USA	Women's professional American football
Gigi Fernandez	Puerto Rico	Tennis

— THE FEDERAL MARRIAGE AMENDMENT —

On Wednesday 15 July 2004, the Federal Marriage Amendment was killed in the United States Senate when a procedural vote to move the measure to the Senate floor for final consideration failed by a 48–50 vote. Supporters of the bill needed 12 more votes to achieve a total of 60. The two Senators who abstained were Democratic Presidential candidate John Kerry (D-Massachusetts) and Democratic Vice-Presidential candidate John Edwards (D-North Carolina). The proposed amendment read as follows:

'Marriage in the United States shall consist only of the union of a man and a woman. Neither this constitution nor the constitution of any State, nor State or Federal law, shall be construed to require that marital status or the legal incidents thereof be conferred upon unmarried couples or groups.'

— THE BABES OF BROOKSIDE —

In 1993, UK TV's *Brookside*, a Channel 4 programme that depicted the mean and gritty life of a Liverpool housing estate, was the first British soap opera to screen lesbian characters as leading parts. The passionate kiss between Beth (Anna Friel) and Margaret, two young and pretty women, was screened 30 minutes before the primetime slot of 9pm. More recently (1999–present), a second lesbian couple, Linsday Corkhill (Claire Sweeney) and Shelley Bowers (Alexandra Westcourt), was introduced. The latter tried to bed her lover's mother in 2000, while Shelley's jealous ex-girlfriend, Paula, was determined to win her back.

— THE DIVINE MISS M ON TOUR —

1970–72: Bette plays on and off at the Continental Baths accompanied by then-unknown Barry Manilow at the piano.

1971–72: 'Bette Midler In Concert' • Johnny Carson's opening act in the Conga Room at the Sahara Hotel in Las Vegas.

1972: Bette receives a two-minute standing ovation when she walks out on stage at Carnegie Hall • Bette ushers in 1973 at New York's Philharmonic Hall wearing a diaper.

1973: 'The Divine Miss M Tour' • cross-country tour to New York's Palace Theater • closes first act of show by walking down a glittery mammoth platform shoe against a New York-skyline backdrop.

1975: 'Clams On The Half Shell Revue' at New York's Minskoff Theater • Overture to *Oklahoma!* is followed by Bette emerging out of a giant clam stuck in a fisherman's net while singing 'Moon Of Manakoora' and performing mid-song with poi balls • Lionel Hampton featured in solo spot and duet with Bette.

1976: 'The Depression Tour' • *Songs For The New Depression* album, featuring an imaginary phone call to 'Mr Rockefeller'.

1977: *Live At Last* album, recorded in Cleveland during 1976 tour.

1977–78: 'An Intimate Evening With Bette', a six-city tour to promote her *Broken Blossom* album • Bette sings Edith Piaf classic 'La Vie en Rose' • plays smaller clubs including the Roxy in Los Angeles.

1978: *The Rose* live in concert at the Wiltern Theater, Los Angeles, on 23 June 1978 • two film shoots at 1pm and 7pm • performs to hundreds of extras cheering for 'Rose!' • World tour that autumn, including five sold-out concerts at London Palladium • two-month tour to Australia, Sweden, France, Belgium, Denmark and Germany • travels serve as an inspiration for her book, *A View From A Broad* • *Bette Midler: Ol' Red Hair Is Back* wins Bette her first of three Emmys for Outstanding Special Comedy, Variety or Music.

1979–80: 'Bette! Divine Madness' tour featuring classic material, comedy bits and new selections from *Thighs And Whispers* album • concert film by same name is shot at Pasadena Theater • Midler is sick, so parts of the film are re-shot on an LA soundstage.

1983:   'De Tour' • Bette promotes her *No Frills* album, featuring 'Beast Of Burden' duet with Mick Jagger • seven-month tour of United States and Canada • last two months of tour filmed in Minnesota for HBO special *Art Or Bust*, which airs in 1984.

1985:   *Mud Will Be Flung Tonight!* comedy album, recorded at the Improv in Los Angeles • Bette disses LaToya Jackson, Bruce Springsteen, Prince and Madonna in her routine.

1993:   'Experience The Divine' tour, her first concert tour in ten years, to promote her *Experience The Divine* greatest-hits album • tour includes six-week stint at Radio City Music Hall • album includes recording of 'One For The Road' (with special lyrics) from her Emmy-winning performance as Johnny Carson's last guest on *The Tonight Show* on 21 May 1992.

1997:   Live concert performance *Divas Las Vegas*, broadcast on HBO, wins Bette her third Emmy for Outstanding Performance in a Variety or Music Programme.

1999:   32-city 'Divine Miss Millennium' tour including New Year's Eve performance at Mandalay Bay, Las Vegas • also known as the 'Bathouse Betty' tour to promote album of the same name.

2003:   'Kiss My Brass' tour kicks off in Chicago, featuring songs from her Grammy-nominated album *Bette Midler Sings The Rosemary Clooney Songbook*, produced by Barry Manilow • tour includes a mixture of old and new material.

— BY US, FOR US: THE FIRST COMMERCIAL — LESBIAN MOVIE

In April 1986, Donna Deitch premiered her film *Desert Hearts* in New York City. Based on Jane Rule's novel *Desert Of The Heart*, it was the first lesbian-produced movie about lesbians to be released commercially. The film is now considered a classic and big bucks can be asked for the hard-to-find copies sold on eBay.

35

— LESBIAN-FRIENDLY SINGERS —

Horse
Bonnie Raitt
Janis Ian
Joan Armatrading
Natalie Merchant
Phranc
Shawn Colvin
The Butchies
Indigo Girls
kd lang
PJ Harvey
Sinéad O'Connor
Tanita Tikaram
Tracy Chapman
Ani di Franco
Melissa Etheridge
Morcheeba
Sarah McLachlan
Sixpence None The Richer
Tatu

— THE LOVE THAT DARE NOT SPEAK ITS NAME —

Bisexual/gay stars of the silent screen:

- **Nils Asther (1897–1981)** – Bisexual Danish actor raised in Sweden who starred opposite Greta Garbo in *The Wild Orchids* (1929) and *The Single Standard* (1929).

- **J Walter Kerrigan (1879–1947)** – Matinée screen idol who was nicknamed 'the Gibson Man' because he was as handsome as the Gibson Girl (the ideal woman of the early 1900s, named after her creator, illustrator Charles Gibson). He retired from showbusiness after appearing as a Western hero in *The Covered Wagon* and playing the title character in the silent version of *Captain Blood*.

- **Ramon Novarro (1899–1968)** – Romantic leading man best known for playing the title role in the silent version of *Ben-Hur*. His career fizzled with the coming of sound, although he did make further occasional appearances. In 1968, Novarro was brutally murdered in his Hollywood home by two young men.

- **Eugene O'Brien (1880–1966)** – Rugged leading man who starred opposite Norma Talmadge in 11 melodramas. Like many silent-movie actors, he didn't survive the transition to sound.

— IN OTHER WORDS: A LESBIAN BY —
ANY OTHER NAME...

LANGUAGE	WORD	TRANSLATION
Spanish	*mal-flor/manflora*	Tomboy
Spanish	*Marimacho*	masculine Mary
Spanish	*Pantalonuda*	tomboy, trouser-wearer
Spanish	*Donna con Donna*	Woman with woman
German	*Mädchen Schmeker*	Girl-taste
Klamath Tribe	*sawa linaa*	To live as partners
Mexican	*Tortillera*	Tortilla maker
French	*Vrille*	A gimlet
Chinese	*Dui shi*	Paired eating (term for female homosexual couples, not cunnilingus)
Hindi	*Shanda/shandali*	A woman desiring like a man; a woman having the properties of a man, etc
Hindi	*Samlaingikta*	Homosexuality
NATIVE AMERICAN		
Cheyenne	*Heemaneh*	Half-men, half-women
Pueblo of Zuni	*Katsotse*	Boy-girl
Shoshoni	*Tainna wa'ippe*	Man-woman

— COUNTRIES IN WHICH SAME-SEX RELATIONSHIPS —
ARE RECOGNISED FOR IMMIGRATION PURPOSES

Australia • Belgium • Canada • Denmark • Finland • Germany • Iceland • The Netherlands • New Zealand • Norway • South Africa • Sweden • United Kingdom

— JUDGE MORGAN —

Mary Morgan was appointed to the San Francisco
Municipal Court on 26 August 1981 by Governor
Jerry Brown, making her the first openly lesbian
judge in America.

— THE TROUBLE WITH *SOAP* —

Soap was a popular sitcom that aired on US channel ABC for four
seasons between 1977 and 1981. Before it even hit the airwaves,
this satire on soap operas was targeted by right-wing groups, who
demanded the network pull it from their fall schedule. The protestors
had read a *Newsweek* article describing the show's characters and
plots, which contained subject matter (infidelity, murder,
homosexuality) considered by some as inappropriate for primetime
viewing. ABC reportedly received 20,000 letters before the show
debuted.

Their primary target was gay character Jodie Dallas (played by Billy
Crystal), who in the first few episodes planned to have a sex-change
operation so he could be with his lover, closeted pro-football player
Dennis Phillips (played by Olympic pole vaulter Bob Seagren). Crystal
initially portrays Jodie as a stereotypical, swishy queen. Perhaps
responding to the complaints of right-wingers and gay activists, the
latter of whom were also not pleased with the character (but for
different reasons), Jodie's limp wrist later disappeared, but so did
Dennis. For the remainder of the series, Jodie was without a boyfriend
and his storylines all involved women: Alice (Randee Heller), his
lesbian roommate; Carol David (Rebecca Balding), a man-trap who
seduces Jodie; and Wendy, his baby daughter, who is the result of
Jodie's one and only heterosexual experience.

— CANTONESE GROIN PLANT —

Chinese medieval literature is said to have referred
to a plant shaped like a phallus with the incredible
property that, when soaked in hot water, it
expanded and hardened and was therefore often
used as a dildo.

— I'M NOT GAY. REALLY. —

The following celebrities have denied that they are gay or lesbian. Here's what they said:

'I am not gay.'   *– Benny Hill, 1982*

'Who might think that with this demeanour, I could be gay? Do I talk like them? Do I move like them?'
– Mel Gibson, 1991

'I am not gay. I am however, thin, single and neat.'
– Jerry Seinfeld, 1993, in his autobiography, Sein Language

'We are heterosexual and monogamous and take our commitment to each other very seriously. Reports of a divorce are totally false. We remain very married. We both look forward to having a family. Marriage is hard enough without all these negative speculations.'
– Newspaper ad taken out by Richard Gere and Cindy Crawford, 1994

'I am not in the closet. I am not coming out of the closet. I am not gay.'
– Oprah Winfrey, 1997

'I'm not a lesbian. I wish they'd stop saying it. I have a daughter, for God's sake. What do they mean by this? They write this shit and one day I'm gonna have to talk to my daughter.'
– Whitney Houston, 1995

'You know, when you don't go on TV and talk about how many women you sleep with, some people in Hollywood that are supposedly "in the know" start whispering that you're gay. If I were gay, I wouldn't be ashamed to admit it, but I'm not.'
– Adam Sandler, 2000

'As it happens, I'm not gay. But I'll certainly let everybody know it if and when I discover that I am.'
– Kenneth Branagh, 2000

'I'm not gay. I'm heterosexual... I can't convince people what to think. I can only say what I know and what the truth is, and that's heterosexual and I date women. That's it. End of story.'
– Mike Piazza (New York Mets), 2002

— THE BIRTH OF CONTEMPORARY LESBIAN POLITICS —

In 1955, Del Martin and Phyllis Lyon started a small group called Daughters of Bilitis (DOB) in San Francisco, the name originating from French author Pierre Louÿs's book *Song Of Bilitis*, which contained love poems between women. DOB was considered to be a subtle enough name for those in the know to understand, but not necessarily obvious enough to 'out' any member if their connection to the group was discovered and revealed. In 1955, the group had eight members, a number that grew substantially over the ensuing years as the group rapidly became one of the few organisations whereby lesbians could meet outside of 'the scene'. Chapters sprang up all over the US and as far afield as Melbourne, Australia.

The Daughters of Bilitis and the (predominantly gay male) Mattachine Society initially worked together in promoting their common queer cause. However, with the growth of the women's liberation movement, it became apparent that the men of Mattachine did not necessarily support the second agenda, that of women's lib. Even the women's libbers were not particularly embracing of the lesbian agenda, with the National Organisation for Women – a prominent feminist organisation – referring to some of their lesbian members as 'the lavender menace'. These schisms showed in the membership of DOB, and its direction was split between those who favoured furthering the lesbian political agenda and those who preferred to champion the rights of women.

The group never really recovered from this fundamental split. However, this cannot undermine the importance of DOB in lesbian political history. Its existence at a time when no other social grouping existed to allow lesbians to get to know one another helped many women to develop a taste for revolutionary sexual politics and paved the way for organisations like the Lesbian Avengers in the 1990s.

Del Martin and Phyllis Lyon got married in San Francisco on 12 February 2004, having been a couple since 1953. The City of San Francisco issued them with the first-ever US same-sex couple, government-sanctioned marriage licence. Go, girls!

— THE RED RIBBON PROJECT —

The Red Ribbon Project was launched in 1991 by the Visual AIDS Artists' Caucus, a New York group of artists dedicated to increasing the public's awareness of AIDS through the arts.

The Caucus chose the red ribbon as a visual symbol of their compassion and solidarity with people living with AIDS. According to Frank Moore, who conceived the ribbon, the colour red was chosen for its 'connection to blood and the idea of passion – not only anger, but love, like a valentine'.

The first celebrity to wear a ribbon on national television was actor Jeremy Irons at the 1991 Tony Awards. Since then, the red ribbon has become an international symbol for AIDS awareness. It has also inspired activists for other social causes to adopt a coloured ribbon as their symbol – for example, a pink ribbon for breast cancer, green for the environment, purple for urban violence.

— RELIGIOUS FANTASY —

Whilst most lesbians escaped legal prosecution through the ages, inevitably some were caught in the act. One such person was a nun, Sister Benedetta Carlini in Pescia, near Florence, who was caught and imprisoned for life sometime around 1619–23. Her crime was not lesbianism but blasphemy, for she claimed as her defence that she had had religious visions that required her cellmate in the nunnery to masturbate her! Not quite 'the devil made me do it', but close…

— CLAUSE 28: A TIMELINE OF EVENTS —

DECEMBER 1987   Conservative MP David Wilshire proposes an amendment to the Local Government Bill that would make it illegal for local authorities to 'promote homosexuality or...promote the teaching in any maintained school of the acceptability of homosexuality'.

9 JANUARY 1988   Opposition to the amendment is quick to mount and a month later more than 10,000 lesbians and gay men demonstrate against Clause 28 in a march through central London.

2 FEBRUARY 1988   Three women protest against Clause 28 by abseiling off the public gallery into the chamber of the House of Lords with shouts of 'Lesbians are angry!'

29 FEBRUARY 1988   Once again, demonstrators take to the streets, this time in Manchester, where between 5,000 and 20,000 participate in a march.

9 MARCH 1988   Clause 28 of the Local Government Bill is approved by the House of Commons and becomes Section 28 of the Local Government Act.

30 APRIL 1988   An estimated 30,000 demonstrators march in London to protest the passage of Clause 28. This is the largest lesbian and gay rally in the history of the UK.

24 MAY 1988   Clause 28 of the Local Government Act takes effect, effectively preventing government from providing any support to pro-lesbian and -gay organisations.

NOVEMBER 2003   Clause 28 is finally removed from the law books.

— GOING DOWN ON LORDS —

In a protest against Clause 28 of the British Local Government Bill (proposed by the Tory Government in 1988 to prohibit local authorities from 'promoting' homosexuality using public funds), a group of lesbians somehow managed to smuggle an abseiling kit into the visitors' gallery of the House of Lords and abseiled down from the gallery to the floor during a key debate on the measure. Some of the same women also broke into the studios of the *BBC Six O'Clock News* in May of the same year and disrupted the live broadcast. Despite the protests, the Bill was passed and became Section 28 of the Local Government Act.

— STICKS AND STONES... —

Here's a list of some of the more colourful derogatory names gay men have been called over the ages:

Brown nose
Butt pirate
Fag
Faggot
Fairy
Fem
Fruit
Homo
Light in the loafers
Limp wrist
Mary
Nancy
Pansy
Pooftah
Queen
Queer
Sausage jockey

— ENGLISH DENIAL OF LESBIANS —

Lesbian sex has never been explicitly prohibited or legalised by the English Parliament, while documentation of homosexual illegality is made with reference to gay male activity involving the acts of fellatio or sodomy. There is no statutory age detailed for lesbian sex, so by default it comes under the same conditions as straight sex. In Europe, most countries set the age somewhere in the early to mid teens, with the age of lesbian consent in Britain and Germany set at 16.

— BISEXUAL/GAY ACADEMY AWARD WINNERS —

The following boys got lucky and took little Oscar home with them on awards night:

Recipient	Award	Film	Year
Peter Allen (songwriter)	Best Music, Original Song, 'Arthur's Theme (The Best That You Can Do)'	Arthur	1981
Pedro Almodóvar	Best Screenplay Written Directly for the Screen	Talk To Her	2003
Howard Ashman (lyricist)	Best Music, Original Song, 'Under The Sea'	The Little Mermaid	1989
	Best Music, Original Song, 'Beauty And The Beast'	Beauty And The Beast	1991
(Ashman died due to AIDS in 1991; his partner, Bill Lauch, accepted the statue on his behalf)			
Alan Ball	Best Screenplay Written Directly for the Screen	American Beauty	2000
Cecil Beaton (designer)	Best Costume, Colour	Gigi	1958
	Best Art Direction – Set Decoration, Colour Best Costume	My Fair Lady	1964
Bruce Cohen (producer)	Best Picture	American Beauty	2000
Bill Condon	Best Screenplay, Based on Material Previously Published or Produced	Gods And Monsters	1998
John Corigliano	Best Music, Original Score	The Red Violin	1998
George Cukor	Best Director	My Fair Lady	1964
Danilo Donato	Best Costume Design	Romeo And Juliet	1968
	Best Costume Design	Casanova	1976
Rob Epstein	Best Documentary, Feature Film	The Times Of Harvey Milk	1984
	Best Documentary, Feature Film	Common Threads: Stories From The Quilt	1989

RECIPIENT	AWARD	FILM	YEAR
Jeffrey Friedman	Best Documentary, Feature Film	*Common Threads: Stories From The Quilt*	1989
Piero Gherardi	Best Costume Design, Black and White	*La Dolce Vita*	1960
	Best Costume Design, Black and White	*8½*	1963
Sir Alec Guinness	Best Actor in a Leading Role	*Bridge Over The River Kwai*	1957
Sir John Gielgud	Best Actor in a Supporting Role	*Arthur*	1981
William Inge	Best Writing, Story and Screenplay Written Directly for the Screen	*Splendor In The Grass*	1962
Paul Jabarra	Best Music, Original Song, 'Last Dance'	*Thank God It's Friday*	1978
Dan Jinks	Best Picture	*American Beauty*	2000
Sir Elton John (composer)	Best Music, Original Song, 'Can You Feel the Love Tonight'	*The Lion King*	1994
Charles Laughton	Best Actor	*The Private Life Of Henry VIII*	1933
Charles LeMaire	Best Costume Design, Black and White	*All About Eve*	1950
	Best Costume Design, Colour	*The Robe*	1950
	Best Costume Design, Colour	*Love Is A Many Splendored Thing*	1953
Orry-Kelly	Best Costume Design, Colour	*An American In Paris*	1951
	Best Costume Design	*Les Girls*	1957
	Best Costume Design, Black and White	*Some Like It Hot*	1959
Dean Pitchford (lyricist)	Best Music, Original Song, 'Fame'	*Fame*	1980
Tony Richardson	Best Picture Best Director	*Tom Jones*	1963
John Schlessinger	Best Director	*Midnight Cowboy*	1969
Robert Schmiechen	Best Documentary, Feature Film	*The Times Of Harvey Milk*	1984

BISEXUAL/GAY ACADEMY AWARD WINNERS
— (CONT'D) —

RECIPIENT	AWARD	FILM	YEAR
Gil Steele	Best Costume Design, Black and White	*The Heiress*	1949
	Best Costume Design, Colour	*Samson And Delilah*	1949
Edward Stevenson	Best Costume Design, Black and White	*The Facts Of Life*	1961

— BORN TO HAND JIVE: AN A–Z OF TERMS FOR —
FEMALE MASTURBATION

The five-digit disco
Applying lip gloss
Basting the tuna
Bouncing the bearded clam
Buzzing the honey hole
Checking the oil
Checking the status of the I/O port
Clam-twiddling jamboree
Cleaning the fur coat
Dialing O on the little pink telephone
Diddling Miss Daisy
Doing the two-finger slot rumba
Entering the ring of fire
Fare un ditolino (Italian: to do a little finger)
Finger blasting
Fingering the fountain
Flossing the cat
Friday-night lip service
Getting a stain out of the carpet
Going mining
Gusset typing
Hula hooping
Itching the ditch
Juicing the clam
Letting your fingers do the walking
Menage à moi
Paddling the pink canoe
Petting the dog

Petting the kitty
Playing solitaire
Pre-heating the oven
Reading in braille
Riding the clitoris-saurus
Romancing thy own
Rubbin' the nubbin
Shooting the rapids
Stiffening the upper lip
Surfing the channel
The two-fingered tango
Tickling the taco
Unclogging the drain
Whipping the nest
Working in the garden
Unbuttoning the fur coat

— 'ALL THE HOMOS FIT TO PRINT' —

The word *lesbian* first appeared in the *New York Times* in a 'Letter To The Editor', signed 'The City Hall-Ringer', in which the male author complained about the English translations of French romance novels that his wife had given him to read. He admitted to liking the later novels of George Sand (a pseudonym for Amandine Aurore Lucie Dupin, who later became Baroness Dudevant), but not her early ones, which he describes as 'true Devil's Literature, worthy of the age of that Lesbian vice, of which Sappho was suspect'.

The word *homosexual* first appeared in the *New York Times* on 22 November 1914 in the second instalment of writer George Bernard Shaw's controversial essay 'Common Sense About the War'. Here, the author states his reasons for opposing Britain's involvement in World War I, making a reference to 'the 40 tolerated homosexual brothels of Berlin'. However, the word did not appear again until 1923. (Four years later, the word *homosexuality* made its first appearance in the newspaper.)

The *New York Times* first substituted the term *gay men* for *homosexuals* on 15 July 1987 in an article about the effects of AIDS on San Francisco and the Castro district. The article explains, '2,030 people, all of them gay men, have died of the disease…'

— BOSTON MARRIAGE —

This term was used to describe a monogamous household relationship between two cohabiting women (particularly used on the American East Coast and, more specifically, New England). It began to appear in the mid 19th century as women's education increased and their economic statuses enabled them to live without the financial support that marriage to a man had previously brought.

Estimates suggest that up to half of the graduating women of this time didn't marry, in part due to most men fearing educated females and not daring to take them as wives, but also as a result of women finding kindred spirits in their college friends – other women who shared their dreams and aspirations. For the first time, Boston Marriages provided the possibility for middle-class women to be economically independent of their families.

Emotional commitment in these relationships was well recognised, but whether they were sexual or not is not definitively known. What *is* known, however, is that they were often clearly love-centred. Boston Marriages were considered completely normal, although not on a par with real (ie heterosexual) marriages. Authors such as Henry James, in *The Bostonians*, depicted society's level of comfort with the concept at the time.

— LITTLE JOE NEVER GAVE IT AWAY... —

Actors who have played male hustlers in feature films:

ACTOR	CHARACTER	FILM	YEAR
Kevin Bacon	Ricky	*Forty Deuce*	1982
	Willie O'Keefe	*JFK*	1991
Joe Dallesandro	Joe	*Flesh*	1968
David Arquette	John	*Johns*	1996
Lukas Haas	Donner	*Johns*	1996
Robert La Tourneaux	Cowboy	*Boys in the Band*	1970
River Phoenix	Max Waters	*My Own Private Idaho*	1991
Jonathan Taylor Thomas	Steve	Speedway Junky	1999
Jon Voight	Joe Buck	*Midnight Cowboy*	1969

— LESBIAN AND BISEXUAL WOMEN OF 1920s HARLEM —

Bessie Smith (blues singer, Ma Rainey's protégée)
Gladys Bentley (singer, self-identified 'bulldagger')
Jackie 'Moms' Mabley (comedian, singer, actress)
Alberta Hunter (vaudeville and cabaret performer, blues diva)
Gertrude 'Ma' Rainey (the Mother of the Blues, singer)
Joséphine Baker (exotic entertainer, dancer)
Ethel Waters (jazz singer, actress)

— GAY BUMPER STICKERS —

I'm not gay but my boyfriend is
Homophobia is a social disease
Anita Bryant like Anita hole in my head
I can't even think straight
My sexual orientation? Horizontal, usually
Let's get one thing straight: I'm not
Straight but not narrow
Equal rights are not special rights
Pink sheep of the family
Doing my part to piss off the radical right
It's only kinky the first time
2QT2BSTR8
Hate is not a family value
Jerry Falwell can suck my Tinky Winky
Mom knows
Who's your daddy?

— LESBIANS AND RELIGIOUS LAW —

Neither the Old Testament, the New Testament nor the Koran has anything to say about lesbianism or it being a sin. The closest these tracts get to condemning same-sex relationships is in Leviticus 20:13 and 18:22, where mention is made only of man lying down with man as being sinful. Because of this omission, lesbians have often escaped the punishments endured by gay men due to the mere absence of any law to invoke!

— INTRODUCTION TO GAY FICTION —

'There's no such thing as a moral or an immoral book. Books
are well written or badly written.'
— *Oscar Wilde*

Here's an alphabetical list of gay and gay-themed books. They are all very
well written. Oscar would have been pleased.

Bertram Cope's Year (1919) – Henry Blake Fuller
Billy Budd (1924) – Herman Melville
A Boy's Own Story (1982) – Edmund White
Brideshead Revisited (1945) – Evelyn Waugh
The Buddha Of Suburbia (1990) – Hanif Kureishi
The City And The Pillar (1948) – Gore Vidal
City Of Night (1963) – John Rechy
Confessions Of A Mask (1949) – Yukio Mishima
The Confusions Of Young Törless (1906) – Robert Musil
Dancer From The Dance (1978) – Andrew Holleran
Death In Venice (1912) – Thomas Mann
Ernesto – Umberto Saba (written in 1953;
published posthumously in 1976)
The Front Runner (1974) – Patricia Nell Warren
Giovanni's Room (1956) – James Baldwin
A Home At The End Of The World (1990) – Michael Cunningham
In A Shallow Grave (1975) – James Purdy
Kiss Of The Spider Woman (1976) – Manuel Puig
The Lost Language of the Cranes (1986) – David Leavitt
Maurice – EM Forster (written in 1913; revised 1920, 1932, 1959;
published posthumously in 1971)
The Mysteries Of Pittsburgh (1988) – Michael Chabon
Mysterious Skin (1995) – Scott Heim
Other Voices, Other Rooms (1948) – Truman Capote
Our Lady Of The Flowers (1942) – Jean Genet
The Picture Of Dorian Gray (1890–91) – Oscar Wilde
Queer (1985) – William Burroughs
Remembrance Of Things Past (1913–27) – Marcel Proust
A Single Man (1964) – Christopher Isherwood
The Swimming Pool Library (1988) – Alan Hollinghurst
Tales Of The City (1978) – Armistead Maupin
Wings (1906) – Mikhail Alekseevich Kuzmin
The Young And The Evil (1933) – Charles Henri Ford and Parker Tyler

— EXECUTED FOR LADY-LOVE —

It's a common misconception that there have been no laws against lesbianism anywhere. Although it may be true for England and America, in Europe, before the French Revolution, lesbian acts were regarded as legally equivalent to those of male sodomy, which were punishable by death.

The earliest legal reference to lesbians seems to be the 1260 French law code *Li Livres di Jostice et de Plet* mandating punishment for women (and men) who commit same-sex acts. For women, the first and second offence curiously resulted in removal of 'the member', which has latterly been taken to mean the clitoris first, followed by the breasts. The third offence for both genders was burning at the stake. No prosecutions under this law are known, although records suggest that the possibility of such a punishment was a part of popular imagination.

- Perhaps the earliest recorded lesbian execution took place in Speier in 1477, when a girl was drowned for lesbian love.

- In the 16th century, two Spanish nuns were executed and women in Granada were whipped and sent to the gallows, in both instances for using 'sexual instruments'.

- A passing woman from Fontaines was burned alive in around 1535, and a weaver named Marie was hanged in 1580, in each case for dressing as a man and marrying a woman, using a 'device' for intercourse.

- In 1549, a woman was banished from Saragosa, in Aragon, for 'imperfect sodomy' (unnatural sexual relations without penetration by a penis); and a lesbian in Geneva in 1568 was put to death by drowning for the same crime.

- The lesbian Isabel Galandre was burned as a witch at Neuchâtel in 1623. (One wonders whether or not her 'members' were *in situ* at the time of her death...)

— DYKES ON BIKES —

No Gay Pride march is complete without those thumping Harleys and their leather-clad, bare-breasted beauties that usually lead out the parade to loud cheers and the air of expectation. Australia's Sydney Mardi Gras is said to have the finest representation of the species.

BISEXUAL AND GAY QUEENS
— WHO HAVE BEEN KNIGHTED —

Sir Hardy Amies (1909–2003), fashion designer and Queen Elizabeth II's dressmaker

Sir Frederick Ashton (1904–88), dancer/choreographer

Sir Francis Bacon (1561–1626), philosopher/scientist/essayist

Sir James M Barrie (1860–1937), writer (*Peter Pan*)

Sir Cecil Beaton (1904–80), photographer/set and costume designer

Sir Michael Bishop (born 1942), Chairman, BMI British Midland Airlines

Sir Dirk Bogarde (1921–99), actor

Sir Cecil Maurice Bowra (1898–1970), literary critic

Sir Benjamin Britten (1913–76), composer

Sir Richard Francis Burton (1821–90), explorer

Sir Richard Casement (1864–1916), civil servant

Sir Noël Coward (1899–1973), playwright/composer/performer

Sir William Dobell (1899–1970), Australian artist

Sir Anthony Dowell (born 1943), ballet dancer/artistic director of the Royal Ballet

Sir Adrian Fulford (born 1953), lawyer/judge

Sir Alec Guinness (1914–2000), actor

Sir Norman Hartnell (1901–79), fashion designer

Sir Nigel Hawthorne (1929–2001), actor

Sir Elton John (born 1947), singer/songwriter

Sir Hector Macdonald (1853–1903), general

Sir Ian McKellen (born 1939), actor

Sir Harold Nicholson (1886–1968), diplomat/writer

Sir Maurice Oldfield (1915–81), Director General, British Secret Service

Sir Laurence Olivier (1907–89), actor

Sir Peter Pears (1910–86), tenor

Sir Stephen Spender (1909–95), writer/critic

Sir Arthur Sullivan (1842–1900), librettist

Sir Michael Kemp Tippet (1905–98), composer

Sir Francis Walsingham (*circa* 1530–90), statesman

Sir Angus Wilson (1913–91), ambassador

— BIRDS BEHIND BARS —

Caged lesbian liaisons have been depicted for decades in popular prison films and TV drama. Here's a quick look at some memorable pink-screen moments:

- The 1950s film *Caged* was directed by John Cromwell and tells the story of a young woman (Eleanor Parker) who, while doing time, is corrupted into lesbianism by a lecherous vice queen, Elvira (Lee Patrick). In the film, the pair are tormented and watched over by a sadistic matron (Hope Emerson).

- *Prisoner: Cell Block H* was first screened in 1979 in Australia and became a cult TV show. Set in the all-women environs of Wentworth Detention Centre, the programme detailed the lives of women on the inside and became a smash-hit series that was subsequently shown in 40 countries worldwide in 12 different languages.

  Many characters in the show became household names, providing dyke pin-ups for the decade:

  - 'Queen Bea' (Val Lehman), the brutish-but-fair boss of the broads;

  - Judy Bryant (Betty Bobbitt), a demon on the steam-press, who committed her crime to ensure that she was banged up with her lover, Sharon;

  - Joan 'The Freak' Ferguson (Maggie Kirkpatrick), the malicious, hardened screw who everyone loathed and who had beaten up the prisoner who had killed her lover;

  - Meg (Elspeth Ballantyne), a good and fair screw, loved by all, who offset the angst of Ferguson and was a veritable soft touch.

  - All are looked over by Superintendent Erica 'Davo' Davidson (Patsy King), the fist of iron and ruler of the roost.

  This series propelled the song 'Over The Rainbow' into a dyke classic and a perennial slow-dance number at lesbian dos.

— BIRDS BEHIND BARS (CONT'D) —

- *Women In Prison* (1987–88) was a US sitcom set in a women's prison, where prisoner Bonnie (Antoinette Byron) is an English hooker who happens to be a lesbian.

- In Britain, the popular TV drama *Bad Girls* (1999–current) is a thrilling drama taking a political stance for imprisoned women, remaining a landmark in depiction of love between women on TV. An award-winning production (Best Drama at the National Television Awards, 2000/2001) drawing 9 million viewers at its peak, it was the first mainstream series to feature two main heroines as lesbians, soulmates on the opposite sides of the fence.

  - Nikki (Mandana Jones) is a passionate but principled convict who has been sentenced for killing the policeman who tried to rape her girlfriend. A hard nut with a soft centre, she is mistrusting of officers and is viewed by them as a trouble-maker.

  - Helen (Simone Lahbib) is a rule-bound wing governor at Larkhall who is determined to do good and eventually befriends Nikki. Their attraction ultimately becomes sexual.

  - Youngster Denny Blood (Alycia Eyo) was influenced and manipulated by her first prison lover, Shell Dockley, but then developed a relationship with Shaz Wylie (Lindsay Fawcett), who later died in a fire that ripped through Larkhall.

  - Selena Geeson (Charlotte Lucas), a basic officer, joined the prison service to be with her girlfriend, Kris Yates (Jennifer Ness), who was sentenced to life for killing her father, although it was later revealed that she was covering up for her younger sister.

— SAPPHO WAS NOT THE ONLY GREEK LESBIAN POET —

On the island of Telos, Greece, in about 400BC, the poet Erinna wrote a long poem bereaving the loss of her beloved Baucis to marriage and to death. Erinna, who died at the age of 19, is one of several Greek women poets whose work – now mostly lost but widely acclaimed in ancient times – included depictions of homo-erotic relationships.

— HOMOPHOBIA HALL OF SHAME: —
US SENATOR RICHARD JOHN 'RICK' SANTORUM

On 7 April 2003, Senator Richard Santorum (R-Pennsylvania) sat down with an Associate Press reporter for an interview. At one point, the reporter asked about his views on homosexuality, gay marriage and the Supreme Court's upcoming decision in the *Lawrence vs Texas* case, which could (and did) overturn the remaining sodomy laws in several states. Here are some of the Senator's more memorable quotes:

- *On homosexuality:* 'I have no problem with homosexuality. I have a problem with homosexual acts. As I would with acts of other, what I would consider to be, acts outside of traditional heterosexual relationships. And that includes a variety of different acts, not just homosexual. I have nothing, absolutely nothing against anyone who's homosexual. If that's their orientation, then I accept that.'

- *On same-sex marriage:* 'In every society, the definition of marriage has not ever to my knowledge included homosexuality. That's not to pick on homosexuality. It's not, you know, man on child, man on dog or whatever the case may be.'

- *On repealing sodomy laws:* 'If the Supreme Court says that you have the right to consensual sex within your home, then you have the right to bigamy, you have the right to polygamy, you have the right to incest, you have the right to adultery. You have the right to anything. Does that undermine the fabric of our society? I would argue yes, it does.'

— CHALKING UP THE PAVEMENT —

In the Campaign for Women's Suffrage Movement of the early 20th century, members would chalk the time and place of a meeting or action to advertise it to other women. (One hopes that they were forgiven by their more militant colleagues – particularly in the rain-enhanced UK – for arriving late as a result of smudged wording!) Later in the same century, women used this popular early-20th-century activist tactic to chalk the outlines of human bodies on pavements, thus marking the spots where women had been raped, while AIDS activists did the same in memoriam of lives lost to the disease.

— GAY ADULT VIDEO NEWS AWARDS —

Since 2001, the Gay Adult Video News Awards have been given out in recognition of excellence in the gay adult-video genre. Here's a list of categories and the 2004 winners:

CATEGORY	2004 WINNER
Best Actor	Michael Soldier, *A Porn Star Is Born*
Best All-Sex Video (tie)	*Bone Island Gorge*
Best Alternative Video	*The Agony Of Ecstasy*
Best Amateur Video	*Mykonos: LKP Casting 3*
Best Art Direction	*Carny*
Best Bisexual Video	*Bisexual Houseguest*
Best Classic DVD	*The Other Side Of Aspen 2*
Best Director	Wash West, *The Hole*
Best Director (Bisexual)	Dirk Yates, *Dirk Yates' Private Collection 208*
Best DVD	*Just For Fun*
Best DVD Extras	*Carny*
Best Editing	Andrew Rosen, *The Hole*
Best Ethnic-Themed Video	*Sins Of The World*
Best Foreign Release	*Legionnaires*
Best Group Scene	Johnny Hazzard, Matt Summers, Logan Reed, Chad Hunt, Matt Majors, Andy Hunter and Mike Johnson, *Detention*
Best Leather Video	*Skuff 2*
Best Music	Gian Franco, *There Goes the Neighborhood*
Best Newcomer	Jason Ridge
Best Non-Sex Performance	Rowdy Carson, *There Goes The Neighborhood*
Best Oral Scene	Brad Patton, Lane Fuller, *Drenched 1*
Best Overall Marketing Campaign	*The Hole*
Best Packaging	*Carny*
Performer of the Year	Joe Foster
Best Renting Tape	*Reload*
Best Screenplay	Rick Tugger, *There Goes The Neighborhood*
Best Sex Comedy	*There Goes The Neighborhood*
Best Sex Scene	Tag Adams and Chad Hunt, *Detention*
Best Solo Performance	Tag Eriksson, *The Hole*
Best Solo Video	*Boywatch 4*
Best Specialty Release	*Mo' Bubble Butt*
Best Specialty Release (18–23)	*American Way 3: Love*

Best Supporting Actor ....Brad Benton, *There Goes The Neighborhood*
Best Threesome ....Michael Vincenzo, Peter Raeg and
Shane Rollins, *Gay Dreams*
Best Video ....*The Hole*
Best Videography ....Bruce Cam, *Gorge*

— THE GAY ADULT VIDEO HALL OF FAME —

Jim Bentley
Kristen Bjorn
Jean-Daniel Cadinot
Bruce Cam
Tom Chase
Gino Colbert
Chip Daniels
Jerry Douglas
George Duroy
Josh Eliot
Joe Gage
Kevin Glover
William Higgins
Ryan Idol
Chad Johnson
Barry Knight
Chi Chi LaRue
Todd Montgomery
Russell Moore
Paul Norman
Johan Paulik
Wakefield Poole
Lukas Ridgeston
Toby Ross
John Rutherford
Ken Ryker
Steven Scarborough
JD Slater
Zak Spears
Derreck Stanton
Jim Steel
Joey Stefano
Matt Sterling

— THE GAY ADULT VIDEO HALL OF FAME (CONT'D) —

Jeff Stryker
John Travis
Kevin Williams
Kurt Young
Daddy Zeus

— COUNTRIES PROVIDING PROTECTION FROM — DISCRIMINATION ON THE BASIS OF SEXUAL ORIENTATION

— SOCARIDES AND 'THE CURE' —

Since the 1960s, Charles Socarides, MD, clinical psychiatrist and former Professor of Psychiatry at Albert Einstein College of Medicine/Montefiore Medical Center in New York City, has advocated that homosexuality is a pathological condition that is treatable. Socarides believes that homosexuality is a learned behaviour, the result of a disturbance during a child's development that prevents him or her from identifying with the parent of the same gender. In 1995, he published *Homosexuality: A Freedom Too Far*, in which he contends that same-sex desire is a neurosis caused by 'smother mothers and abdicating fathers', claiming that through reparative therapy he has helped 35% of his patients become heterosexual. His work is supported by such right-wing groups as Reverend Louis P Sheldon's Traditional Values Coalition, so it's no surprise that he's not a fan of the gay-rights movement, which he alleges endangers 'the primary unit in society, the family'. He also writes that 'AIDS is the same-sex movement's terrifying contribution to this terrific century [*sic*].'

Ironically, Socarides is himself the father of a gay man. In fact, his son, Richard Socarides, is not only openly gay; he was also an advisor to US President Bill Clinton on gay and lesbian issues and served as the White House liaison to the Labor Department.

— WHAT MAKES A LESBIAN? —

Nineteenth-century sexologist Richard von Krafft-Ebing provided a list of attributes that defined the lesbian thus:

- Women with a strong preference for male garments.

- 'The extreme grade of degenerative homosexuality'. The woman of this type, Krafft-Ebing explained, 'possesses of the feminine qualities only the genital organs'.

- Women who 'did not betray their anomaly by external appearance or by mental [masculine] sexual characteristics'. They were, nevertheless, responsive to the approaches of women who appeared or acted more masculine.

- Women whose inversion was 'fully developed' taking on a definitely masculine role.

— FIRST RUSSIAN LESBIAN NOVEL —

In 1907, the Russian bisexual intellectual Lidiya Zinovyeva-Annibal published 33 *Abominations*, the first Russian novel to have lesbianism as its dominant theme.

— ROOMS (AND SEX) BY THE HOUR —

'Buffet flats' were popular after-hours spots in Harlem during the 1920s in what is now called the Harlem Renaissance. They were usually in someone's apartment, and the gin was known to flow freely from whatever vessel came to hand, be it a milk bottle or a baby's bottle.

Essentially private apartments rented by the night, buffet flats first sprang up during the late 1800s to provide overnight accommodation for those black travellers refused service in white-owned hotels. By the 1920s, however, they became somewhat more risqué, playing host to activities ranging from the illegal (such as drinking, gambling and prostitution) right through to a variety of sexual pleasures available 'cafeteria style'. It was in buffet flats that girls got to hang out with other girls, and the bisexual stars of the day such as Bessie Smith or Ma Rainey got to do whatever or whoever they pleased.

— OSCAR HONOURS —

In recent years, films with lesbian content have had tremendous Oscar success in the category Actress in a Leading Role.

The 76th Academy Awards (2004) saw South African Charlize Theron win with her performance in *Monster*, which saw her incredible transformation into the drug-addicted highway prostitute Aileen Wuornos, the real-life serial killer who took her vengeance on men and, in an escalating spree, killed her johns. A love story emerged amidst the horrors, between Wuornos and Selby Wall (played by Christina Ricci), a lesbian sent by her parents to live with her aunt in an attempt to cure her homosexuality. The movie successfully blurs the line between a morally challenged mess and a criminal sociopath.

At the 75th Academy Awards (2003), the award for Best Actress was given to Australian Nicole Kidman for her portrayal of Virginia Woolf in *The Hours*. Starring a trio of the screen's best actresses (Meryl Streep, Julianne Moore and Nicole Kidman), the movie describes a day in the lives of each character, all of whom who are linked by their common yearnings and fears, despite being eras apart. The common thread is Virginia Woolf's first great novel, *Mrs Dalloway*, with each character's engaging story involving a lesbian glimpse, their intertwined stories finally coming together in a surprising moment of shared recognition.

At the 72nd Academy Awards (1999), Hilary Swank won the Best Actress Oscar for her portrayal of the lead character in the movie *Boys Don't Cry*, a true story based on the life of Brandon Teena, a newcomer in Falls City, Nebraska, who had enchanted the small rural community. When it was discovered that this charismatic young stranger was not the person people thought he was, hatred, fuelled by ignorance, saw a young life brutally lost. The heart-breaking, complicated love story of this pre-op transgender woman shattered the heartland in which the abhorrent crime was committed.

Three decades earlier, at the 42nd Academy Awards (1969), Maggie Smith received the Oscar for her role as Jean Brodie, the much-adored teacher of a class of infatuated girls in *The Prime of Miss Jean Brodie*, which pulled on the strong tradition of pupil–teacher infatuations set in the 1930s Weimar Republic with *Mädchen in Uniform*.

There have been several other films with lesbian overtones that have received acclaim at the Academy Awards, winning Oscars in various categories, as tabled below:

Year	Award Category	Recipient	Film
1999	Foreign-Language Film		*All About My Mother*
1995	Foreign-Language Film		*Antonia's Line*
1983	Original Song Score or Adaptation Score	Michel Legrand Alan Bergman Marilyn Bergman	*Yentl*
1982	Actress in a Supporting Role	Jessica Lange	*Tootsie*
1962	Costume Design	Norma Koch	*Whatever Happened To Baby Jane?*
1950	Director	Joseph Mankiewicz	*All About Eve*
1940	Cinematography	George Barnes	*Rebecca*

— THE CASTING COUCH —

Sometimes the actor who creates a role was not necessarily the filmmakers' or the studios' first choice, so just imagine these gay-fave films with the actor initially considered for the leading role:

Film	Role	Imagine...	Instead of...
Mildred Pierce (1945)	Mildred Pierce	Barbara Stanwyck	Joan Crawford
All About Eve (1950)	Margo Channing	Claudette Colbert Gertrude Lawrence	Bette Davis
Sunset Boulevard (1950)	Norma Desmond	Mae West Mary Pickford Pola Negri	Gloria Swanson
A Streetcar Named Desire (1951)	Blanche DuBois	Olivia de Havilland	Vivian Leigh
Some Like It Hot (1959)	Sugar Kane	Mitzi Gaynor	Marilyn Monroe
Who's Afraid Of Virginia Woolf? (1966)	Martha	Ingrid Bergman	Elizabeth Taylor
Moonstruck (1987)	Loretta Castorini	Sally Field	Cher
Fatal Attraction (1987)	Alex Forrest	Debra Winger	Glenn Close

— DYKE SPOTTING —

This is what lesbians do when they're waiting for a bus, pushing a trolley down the shopping aisles, refuelling the car, walking the dog, sitting on the train or just about anything in normal daily routine. It's been dubbed 'having a gaydar' by the boys and is much more interesting than trainspotting. Most dykes reckon they can spot those that bat on the same team through the known, yet invisible, lesbian aether. We note the walk, the fingernail length, the hairdo, the piercings, the kit and the general vibe. 'Clocking' someone will at least produce a smile or wink, occasionally a vocal rendition of the cult classic 'We Are Family', a free drink at the bar or, if you're really lucky, a new girlfriend.

— GAY CLUBS OF 1920s HARLEM —

The Clam House
Lulu Belle's
Hot Cha
Edmond's Cellar

BISEXUAL/GAY MEN 80 YEARS YOUNG
— AND OVER —

Merce Cunningham (born 1919) – dancer/choreographer. His personal and professional relationship with composer John Cage (1912–92) spanned over four decades.

Joseph Hansen (born 1934) – novelist best known for the David Brandsetter mystery series. His first books about gay life were published in the early 1960s under the pseudonym James Colton.

Phillip Johnson (born 1906) – eminent post-modern architect. His list of designs includes the State Theater at Lincoln Center; the Crystal Cathedral in Garden Grove, California; and his Connecticut home, a 'Glass House' he designed for his Masters thesis.

Arthur Laurents (born 1918) – playwright, novelist, screenwriter, librettist and stage director who penned the libretti for *West Side Story*, *Gypsy* and *Hallelujah! Baby*, and the screenplays for *Rope* and *The Way We Were*.

James Purdy (born 1923) – writer. His dark and inventive novels, including *63: Dream Palace* and *In A Shallow Grave*, focus on obsessive love relationships and urban alienation.

Ned Rorem (born 1923) – Pulitzer Prize-winning composer and diarist. *Time* magazine once called him 'the world's best composer of art songs'.

Gore Vidal (born 1925) – novelist, dramatist, social critic and political activist. His credits include one of the first mainstream gay novels, *The City And The Pillar* (1948), and *Myra Breckinridge* (1968).

Franco Zeffirelli (born 1923) – distinguished Italian filmmaker (*Romeo And Juliet*, *Endless Love*, *Tea With Mussolini*), theatre director and production designer. He directed and designed the recent London productions of Pirandello's *Absolutely! (Perhaps)* and *Pagliacci* with Placido Domingo.

— SPARTAN SEX —

The Spartans of around 600BC had a society in which the genders lived separate lives. Women and men commonly had sexual relationships with younger same-sex members of society as an expected part of the younger person's learning and development.

— GAY PORN FILM AUTEURS —

KRISTEN BJORN

Award-winning British-born director who worked briefly as a model in videos (*The New Breed* [1981], *Biker's Liberty* [1982]) before pursuing a career as a photographer for gay magazines. Bjorn's videos are best known for their hunky, (mostly) uncut models; his use of exotic locales (Brazil, Dominican Republic, eastern Europe); and his 'money shots'. His catalogue lists over 30 titles, including *Carnival In Rio* (1989), *Montreal Men* (1993) and *The Vampire Of Budapest* (1995).

GINO COLBERT

Colbert started his porn career as an actor in straight films and moved his way up the ladder to directing straight (*John Wayne Bobbitt – Uncut* [1994]), gay (*Hung And Dangerous* [1991], *Boner* [1992]) and bisexual (*Days Gone Bi* [1988], *Bi-Day, Bi-Night* [1989]) videos. Colbert won a Gay Erotic Video Award and an Adult Video News Award for his co-direction of *Three Brothers* (1998), a film focusing on siblings Vince, Hal and Shane Rockland. He sometimes directs under the pseudonyms 'John Stallion' and 'Sam Schad'.

WILLIAM HIGGINS

The leading gay porn director of the 1980s, Higgins's *oeuvre* includes such classic titles as *Pacific Coast Highway* (1981), *Leo And Lance* (1983) and *Sailor In The Wild* (1983). After losing many of his models to AIDS, Higgins relocated to Amsterdam, where he opened Drakes, a gay club and sex shop. He opened a second club in Prague, where he resumed his directing career in 1997. His Prague films – *Czech by Demand* (1997), *Czech Is In The Male*

(1998), *Prague Buddies* (1998) and *Double Czech* (2000) – which he first started making under the pseudonym 'Wim Hof', feature mostly Czech casts and have militaristic and athletic themes.

Chi Chi Larue (Larry Paciotti)

The 'drag diva of porn', Larue moved from Minnesota to Los Angeles to work in the adult film business, going on to direct over 200 videos and winning numerous directing awards for her work on *The Rise* (1990), *Echoes* (2000) and *Deep South I: The Big And The Easy* (2002). She sometimes works under the pseudonyms 'Lawrence David' and 'Taylor Hudson'.

— GUSHING GIRLS —

Female ejaculation and the G-spot are much mythologised. The G-spot is said to be about 4cm into the vagina, on the contra-lateral side to the clitoris, and has a more sponge-like texture than the surrounding vaginal walls. Stimulation in this area is said to produce a surprising gush of liquid that in no way can be mistaken for the general wetness of good sex. The liquid is clear and watery and for the ejaculator feels not unlike peeing. In itself, female ejaculation is not typically orgasmic, but those who experience it describe it as being a by-product of good sex. Not all women can do it, but those who can, or have excited it in others, have verified its existence.

— THAT CERTAIN SUMMER —

The first US made-for-TV movie about homosexuality was *That Certain Summer*, which debuted on ABC on 1 November 1972. The story focuses on a teenager (Emmy winner Scott Jacoby) who discovers his dad (Hal Holbrook) is gay while visiting him over the summer vacation. *The West Wing*'s Martin Sheen co-starred as Holbrook's lover and Hope Lange played Holbrook's understanding ex-wife.

Most TV critics, along with some gay activists, applauded the film for its non-stereotypical depiction of gay men in a stable relationship – even if ABC prohibited the two men from having any physical contact. Consequently, Holbrook and Sheen seem more like college roommates than lovers.

— BENT POLITICIANS —

Here's a brief rundown of some bisexual/gay/lesbian Members of Parliament:

CURRENT MPs

DAVID BORROW (LABOUR, 1997–)

Borrow came out publicly on 8 June 1998, in the same week as Gordon Marsden. In an interview with *Metropolis* (10 June 1998), Borrow explained that he came out so he can 'raise issues that are important to all lesbians and gay men'.

BEN BRADSHAW (LABOUR, 1997–)

A former BBC Radio correspondent, Bradshaw was one of two MPs (along with Stephen Twigg) to be elected as openly gay candidates. During the 1997 general election, Dr Adrian Rogers sided with Bradshaw's Conservative opponent, stating that this was a contest between 'good and evil' and that homosexuality was 'sterile, disease-ridden and God-forsaken'.

NICK BROWN (LABOUR, 1983–)

Nick Brown was also forced to come out when a former lover offered to sell his story to the *News Of The World*. Brown stated that one of the reasons why he kept his lifestyle private was to avoid upsetting his elderly mother.

CHRIS BRYANT (LABOUR, 2001–)

Although he was a member of the Conservative Party, the members of the Labour Party picked Bryant – a former BBC executive who is openly gay – to represent their constituency of Rhondda.

ALAN DUNCAN (CONSERVATIVE, 1992–)

Duncan was the first Tory to come out to the press of his own accord (in 2002), which put the Conservative Party's history of intolerance to the test.

ANGELA EAGLE (LABOUR, 1992–)

Eagle is the first lesbian MP to come out voluntarily (on 3 September 1997) since Maureen Colquhoun's announcement back in 1976.

GORDON MARSDEN (LABOUR, 1997–)

Marsden came out in June 1998, in the same week as David Borrow.

CHRIS SMITH (LABOUR, 1983–)

In 1984, at a protest rally against a city council that rescinded a non-discrimination policy, Smith came out simply by stating, 'My name is Chris Smith, I'm the Labour MP for Islington South and I'm gay.'

STEPHEN TWIGG (LABOUR, 1997–)
Twigg, along with Ben Bradshaw, was one of the first openly gay MPs to be elected.

FORMER MPs
WILLIAM JOHN BANKES (MP, 1810–34)
Bankes was an art collector, a world traveller and a close friend of Lord Byron. His career in Parliament ended when he was arrested by a police officer for having a sexual liaison with a private in the Royal Guards.

MICHAEL BROWN (CONSERVATIVE, 1979–97)
Brown came out in 1994 when he learned that the *News Of The World* was planning to run photographs of him with a 20-year-old companion vacationing in Barbados. He lost his seat in the May 1997 general election.

MAUREEN COLQUHOUN (LABOUR, 1974–79)
In 1976, Colquhoun admitted that her marriage had ended and she was living with a woman. She lost her seat in the general election of 1979.

RON DAVIES (LABOUR, 1983–2001)
In October 1998, Davies was the victim of a mugging and attempted extortion near a gay cruising spot. A scandal erupted and Davies was forced to come out as bisexual and quit as Labour's candidate to become the first secretary of Wales. He gave up his seat in the 2001 general election.

TOM DRIBERG (INDEPENDENT, 1942–45; LABOUR, 1945–74)
A prominent British gossip columnist and journalist, Driberg liked to cruise public restrooms, had ties with the USSR and is believed to have been a spy for the KGB.

PETER MANDELSON (LABOUR, 1992–)
An experienced politician credited for reviving the Labour Party in the 1990s, Mandelson served as Prime Minister Tony Blair's campaign manager in the 1997 general election. His outing by former MP Matthew Parris on a television news show in 1998 sparked tabloid headlines, although he has kept mum when it comes to discussing his private life.

MATTHEW PARRIS (CONSERVATIVE, 1979–86)
Politician and journalist Parris announced he was gay in his weekly newspaper column. In 1998, he revealed on *Newsnight* that Peter Mandelson was one of two gay current Labour cabinet members.

— BENT POLITICIANS (CONT'D) —

WILLIAM PITT, THE YOUNGER (TORY, 1781–82; PRIME MINISTER, 1783–1801 AND 1804–1806)
Britain's youngest prime minister preferred to spend his time in the company of gentlemen.

HORACE WALPOLE (WHIG, 1741–67)
The son of British Prime Minister (1721–42) Sir Robert Walpole, Horace Walpole is best known for his Neo-Gothic home, Strawberry Hill, and for writing *The Castle Of Otranto*, which is considered to be the first Gothic novel. His lover was poet Thomas Gray.

— DR RUTH'S FORERUNNERS —

In the latter part of the 19th and early 20th century, there was a groundswell of people interested in human sexuality. Many of these tried to define and otherwise categorise the diversity of sexual interest that they found in their investigations, using scientific theorising as the basis for their classification. This burgeoning field led to an abundance of so-called sexologists. Here are a few:

Hirschfeld • Hodann • Lenz • Reich • Marcuse •
Freud • Eulenberg • Krauss • Korber • Rohleder

— ROYALTY —

The daughter of Gustavus II Adolphus and Maria Eleonora of Brandenburg, Christina, Queen of Sweden (1626–89), was just six years old when her father was killed in the Thirty Years War. The country was then ruled by a regent until 17 December 1644, when she assumed personal rule.

More interested in science and art, Queen Christina took little part in politics, electing to abdicate in 1654 in favour of her cousin Karl-Gustav of Pfalz-Zweibrücken and his male descendants. On stepping down, she secretly converted to Catholicism and travelled to Rome, where she soon became the centre of a school of scholars and where she eventually died in 1689.

Queen Christina was reported to be a hermaphrodite, with contemporary accounts unanimously mentioning her masculine qualities. Her only known female partner was Comtesse Ebba Sparre, whom she met in Paris in 1654, after her abdication. The film *Queen Christina* (1932), with Greta Garbo as the lead, was laced with homosexual and lesbian innuendo and blazed the trail for Garbo's later canonisation as a queer icon.

Meanwhile, in England, on succeeding to the English throne in 1702, Queen Anne (1655–1714) was openly affectionate towards at least two women in court. She was childhood friends with Sarah Jennings, who dominated Anne's household for 26 years after her marriage, especially when she became the Duchess of Marlborough. The two women exchanged frequent written communication as Mrs Morley (Anne) and Mrs Freeman (Sarah), meeting with the disapproval of Anne's sister, Queen Mary. The Duchess of Marlborough sat by Anne's side on most State occasions until 1710, when Anne broke with the Marlboroughs for political reasons, after which Sarah's cousin Mrs Abigail Masham became Anne's new favourite, prompting angry and embittered quarrelling with Sarah.

— SWITCH-HITTERS ON CELLULOID —

Bisexual male characters in film:

CHARACTER	ACTOR	MOVIE	YEAR
Wade Lewis	Robert Redford	*Inside Daisy Clover*	1966
The Visitor	Terence Stamp	*Teorema*	1968
Joe	Joe Dallesandro	*Flesh*	1968
		Trash	1970
		Heat	1972
Konrad Ludwig	Michael York	*Something For Everyone*	1970
Dr Daniel Hirsh	Peter Finch	*Sunday, Bloody Sunday*	1970
Brian Roberts	Michael York	*Cabaret*	1972
Maximilian von Heune	Helmut Griem	*Cabaret*	1972

— UP IN SMOKE —

In one of the most appalling acts of destruction of human endeavour, Pope Gregory VII is supposed to have decreed in 1073 that Sappho's works, the world's oldest poetry of lesbian love (and some of the earliest works of lyric poetry), should be destroyed by burning in bonfires in Rome and Constantinople.

— THE ULTIMATE SHOW-TUNE MIX TAPE —

Song	Show	Composer/Lyricist	Performer	Duration
'All That Jazz'	Chicago	(Kander/Ebb)	Chita Rivera	3:13
'If My Friends Could See Me Now'	Sweet Charity	(Coleman/Fields)	Gwen Verdon	3:29
'Adelaide's Lament'	Guys And Dolls	(Loesser)	Faith Prince	3:38
'My Heart Belongs To Daddy'	Leave It To Me	(Porter)	Mary Martin	2:32
'Always True To You In My Fashion'	Kiss Me, Kate	(Porter)	Lisa Kirk	4:00
'Losing My Mind'	Follies	(Sondheim)	Dorothy Collins	3:40
'I Could Have Danced All Night'	My Fair Lady	(Lerner/Loewe)	Julie Andrews	3:28
'Tonight'	West Side Story	(Bernstein/Sondheim)	Carol Lawrence and Larry Kert	3:54
'What I Did For Love'	A Chorus Line	(Hamlisch/Kleban)	Priscilla Lopez	5:41
'As Long As He Needs Me'	Oliver!	(Bart)	Georgia Brown	4:08
'Don't Rain On My Parade'	Funny Girl	(Styne/Merrill)	Barbra Streisand	2:37
'Hello, Dolly'	Hello, Dolly	(Herman)	Carol Channing and Chorus	5:41
'If He Walked Into My Life'	Mame	(Herman)	Angela Lansbury	3:53
'Send In The Clowns'	A Little Night Music	(Sondheim)	Glynis Johns	3:24
'I'm In Love With A Wonderful Guy'	South Pacific	(Rodgers/Hammerstein)	Mary Martin	3:31
'And I'm Telling You I'm Not Going'	Dreamgirls	(Krieger/Eyen)	Jennifer Holliday	4:05
'I Dreamed A Dream'	Les Misérables	(Schönberg/Kretzmer)	Randy Graff	4:13
'Memory'	Cats	(Lloyd Webber/Elliot)	Betty Buckley	3:36
'Don't Cry For Me, Argentina'	Evita	(Webber/Rice)	Patti LuPone	5:20

Song	Show	Composer/Lyricist	Performer	Duration
'Everything's Coming Up Roses'	Gypsy	(Styne/Sondheim)	Ethel Merman	3:06
'The Ladies Who Lunch'	Company	(Sondheim)	Elaine Stritch	4:26
'Lullaby Of Broadway'	42nd Street	(Warren/Dubin)	Jerry Orbach And Co	4:59

Total running time: 86:56

— BANISHED BY BLUE —

During World War II, discharges for homosexuality from the US armed forces were usually printed on blue paper and were known as 'blue discharges'. If you were in receipt of one of these, you could be disqualified from the usual benefits after discharge as well as from even getting a civilian job. A single piece of blue paper could prevent you from enjoying the benefits owed to you as a result of fighting for your country and could change your life forever.

— VENGEANCE BY JURY —

In 1907, Sholem Asch's Yiddische play Got Fun Nekoma (The God Of Vengeance) premiered in Berlin. It told the story of a Jewish girl whose father runs a brothel, but its significance was its inclusion of two sympathetically portrayed lesbian love scenes, among the first in modern European theatre. By 19 December 1922, the play had gained international fame and the first English-language version opened under the title The God Of Vengeance at the Provincetown Playhouse. This also ushered the first lesbian scenes onto the American stage.

The play's notoriety spread to the extent that, by 6 March 1923, it was moved to Broadway. However, this spelled its demise when the show's producer, the theatre owner and 12 cast members were arrested and charged with 'presenting an obscene, indecent, immoral and impure theatrical production'. A jury ruled against banning the play two months later, but the verdict was later overturned on appeal.

— FIRST RECORDED USE OF THE WORD 'LESBIAN' — IN A SEXUAL CONTEXT

A commentator in the Byzantine Empire, in around AD914, explained that, in referring to 'women who act like men', the second-century Christian theologian Clement of Alexandria meant those women who are 'abominable tribades hetairistriai, or Lesbiai'. This makes it the earliest recorded usage of the term in a context that refers to same-sex acts rather than as residents of Lesbos.

— COVER YOUR EARS! —

Here are some of the dumbest things ever said or written about homosexuality:

- 'Thou shalt not lie with mankind as with womankind; it is an abomination.'
  — Leviticus 18:22

- 'Who are the beneficiaries of the Court's protection? Members of various minorities including criminals, atheists, homosexuals, flag burners, illegal immigrants (including terrorists), convicts, and pornographers.'
  — Pat Buchanan

- 'Many of those people involved in Adolf Hitler were Satanists, many were homosexuals – the two things seem to go together.'
  — Pat Robertson

- 'To hold that the act of homosexual sodomy is somehow protected as a fundamental right would be to cast aside millennia of moral teaching.'
  — Warren E Burger

- 'If homosexuality was the normal way, God would have made Adam and Bruce.'
  — Anita Bryant

- 'I don't think homosexuality is normal behaviour, and I oppose the codification of gay rights.'
  — US President George Bush, 1980

- 'I think marriage is a sacred institution between a man and a woman.'
  – US President George W Bush, 2004

- 'AIDS is not just God's punishment for homosexuals; it is God's punishment for the society that tolerates homosexuals.'
  — *Jerry Falwell, 1993*

- '...Marijuana leads to homosexuality, the breakdown of the immune system, and therefore to AIDS.'
  — *US Drugs czar Carleton Turner, 1986*

- 'I don't mind the homosexuality. I understand it. Nevertheless, goddamn, I don't think you glorify it on public television...even more than you glorify whores. We all know we have weaknesses. But, goddammit, what do you think that does to kids?'
  — *US President Richard Nixon, 1971*

— LESBIAN LITERATURE —

Looking for something to cuddle up with on a winter's night? Here is a non-definitive list of 40 lesbian-authored or -themed books that can be considered pioneering or classic works in that now-widespread phenomenon of the lesbian book.

TITLE	AUTHOR
Aquamarine	Carol Anshaw
Autobiography Of A Family Photo	Jacqueline Woodson
Bastard Out Of Carolina	Dorothy Allison
Cheri	Colette
Death Comes For The Archbishop	Willa Cather
In Thrall	Jane Delynn
La Batarde	Violette Leduc
Les Guerrilleres	Monique Wittig
Little Women	Louisa May Alcott
Lover	Bertha Harris
Miss Peabody's Inheritance	Elizabeth Jolley
Mrs Dalloway	Virginia Woolf
Mrs Stevens Hears The Mermaids Singing	May Sarton
Nightwood	Djuna Barnes
Olivia	Dorothy Bussy
On Strike Against God	Joanna Russ
Oranges Are Not The Only Fruit	Jeanette Winterson
Orlando	Virginia Woolf
Patience And Sarah	Isabel Miller

— LESBIAN LITERATURE (CONT'D) —

Rat Bohemia ....Sarah Schulman
Riverfinger Women ....Elana Nachman/Dykewomon
Rubyfruit Jungle...Rita Mae Brown
Sister Gin ....June Arnold
Sita ....Kate Millett
The Autobiography Of Alice B Toklas ....Gertrude Stein
The Changelings..Jo Sinclair
The Child Manuela (Mädchen In Uniform) ....Christa Winsloe
The Children's Crusade ....Rebecca Brown
The Color Purple..Alice Walker
The Friendly Young Ladies ....Mary Renault
The Heart Is A Lonely Hunter ....Carson McCullers
The Memoirs Of Hadrian ....Marguerite Yourcenar
The Passion...Jeanette Winterson
The Persian Boy...Mary Renault
The Price Of Salt ....Patricia Highsmith
The Well Of Loneliness ....Radclyffe Hall
Therese And Isabelle...Violette Leduc
Three Lives..Gertrude Stein
Two Serious Ladies...Jane Bowles
Zami ....Audre Lorde

— BY ANY OTHER NAME... —

Here's a list of pseudonyms and one-word names used by some famous bisexual and gay men:

Adrian (Hollywood costume designer) ....Adrian Adolph Greenberg (1903–59)

Bruce of Los Angeles (photographer).......................Bruce Harry Bellas (1909–74)

Numa Numantius (author)...................................Karl Heinrich Ulrichs (1825–95)

Orry-Kelly (designer)...John Kelly (1897–1964)

Charlotte von Mahlsdorf (German transvestite).........Lother Berfelde (1928–2002)

Ondine (poet/Warhol superstar) ....Robert Olivio (1937–89)

Rosa von Praunheim (Latvia-born film director)....Holger Mischwitki (born 1942)

Tom of Finland (artist)...Touko Laaksonen (1920–91)

Il Sodoma (Italian Renaissance painter)........Giovanni Antonio Bazzi (1477–1549)

— MEDIEVAL PERSECUTIONS —

There were ten known persecutions of lesbians in 16th-century Europe:

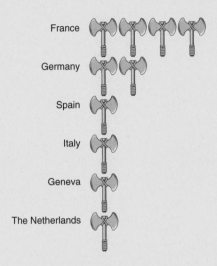

— THE REAL NAMES OF THE LADIES WE LOVE —

You probably know her as ****. Betcha didn't know her real name is ****.

THE STAR	HER REAL NAME
Linda Evans	Linda Evenstad
Diane Keaton	Diane Hall
Carole King	Carole Klein
Patti LaBelle	Patricia Louise Holte
Cleo Laine	Clementina Dinah Campbell
Edith Piaf	Edith Giovanna Gassion
Donna Reed	Donna Belle Mullenger
Joan Rivers	Joan Alexandra Molinsky
Ginger Rogers	Virginia Katherine McMath
Susan Sarandon	Susan Tomaling
Raquel Welch	Racquel Tejada

— HOMOPHOBIA HALL OF SHAME: —
DR LAURA SCHLESSINGER

Laura Schlessinger, PhD, is the controversial host of her own radio call-in programme, *The Dr Laura Show*, which has been nationally syndicated in the US since 1994. Schlessinger has been criticised for her frank, no-nonsense interpersonal style and her penchant for giving callers her own moral opinions on matters related to relationships, marriage, family and child-raising. Her critics believe that the title of her programme is deceptive (she refers to herself as 'Doctor' Laura, yet she holds a PhD in physiology, not psychology). She also claims to be 'licensed marriage, family and child counsellor', yet her licence is no longer active in the State of California. Over the years, Schlessinger has been targeted by gay activists, who succeeded in getting sponsors to pull out of her low-rated, short-lived TV talk show because of her views about homosexuality:

- *On homosexuality:* 'I'm sorry – hear it one more time, perfectly clear: If you're gay or lesbian, it's a biological error that inhibits you from relating normally to the opposite sex. The fact that you are intelligent, creative and invaluable is all true. The error is in your ability to relate sexually intimately, in a loving way, to a member of the opposite sex. It is a biological error.' (8 December 1998)

- *On gay rights:* '[Gay] rights. Rights! *Rights?* For sexual deviant...sexual behaviour there are now rights. That's what I'm worried about with the paedophilia and the bestiality and the sado-masochism and the cross-dressing. Is this all going to be "rights" too, to deviant sexual behaviour? It's deviant sexual behaviour. Why does deviant sexual behaviour get rights? Don't understand that to start out with.' (9 June 1999)

- *On the so-called 'homosexual agenda':* 'When we have the word *homosexual*, we are clarifying the dysfunction, the deviancy, the reality. We change it to the word *gay*, and it makes it more difficult to pinpoint the truth. So one of the things that the homosexual agenda did was to change the name. Just like somebody complained to me yesterday that *ethnic cleansing*...that it sounded like your washing machine, as opposed to murder – and they were right; *ethnic cleansing* sounds nice. *Murder* is the truth. Well, *homosexuality* is the truth. *Gay* isn't.' (12 August 1999)

— NAUGHTY NUNS —

It was long suspected by common folk that the same-sex monastic enclaves of nunneries and monasteries harboured all manner of transgressions against common decency. In an attempt to mitigate against public suspicions (and their own), the councils of Paris in 1212 and Rouen in 1214 stopped nuns from sleeping in the same bed (and, sometimes, even in the same dorm) and ordered for a lamp to be burning all night to ensure that nuns weren't slipping from room to room or from bed to bed!

— NOT A DRAG —

Advertising tag lines to ten drag films:

Connie And Carla (2004): 'When you follow your dream, there's no telling what you'll become'

Flawless (1999): 'Nobody's perfect. Everybody's flawless'

Hedwig And The Angry Inch (2001): 'An anatomically incorrect rock odyssey'

Paris Is Burning (1990): 'Having a ball…wish you were here'

Priscilla, Queen Of The Desert (1994): 'Finally, a comedy that will change the way you think, the way you feel and, most importantly, the way you dress'

La Cage Aux Folles (1978): 'Some like it not'

Some Like It Hot (1959): 'The movie too HOT for words!'

To Wong Foo, Thanks For Everything! Julie Newmar (1995): 'Attitude is everything'

Victor/Victoria (1982): 'The surprise disguise of the year'

Wigstock: The Movie (1995): 'A celebration of life, liberty and the pursuit of big hair!'

— RADCLYFFE HALL: PROTOTYPE FOR —
THE 'MANNISH LESBIAN'

John (Marguerite) Radclyffe Hall (1886–1943) is perhaps one of the world's most famous lesbians as a result of writing the notorious, groundbreaking and best-selling *The Well Of Loneliness* (1928). The book was a bombshell at the time and was considered by many as the Lesbian Bible.

Hall's story tells of protagonist Stephen Gordon, a well-off, horse-riding tomboy who is sexually enlightened, though abusively, by Angela Crossby. After embarking on a literary career, Stephen begins an affair with a girl called Mary, and their relationship forms the core of the text. The role differentiation between Stephen's butch and Mary's femme is extensively explored, with Stephen engulfed throughout, by pessimism and self-pity, about her sexuality. The story concludes with Stephen renouncing Mary to a male partner in order that Mary can lead a 'normal' life. Today's readers will find the work somewhat dated, with Hall subscribing to the then-popular theories of 'sexual inversion' and the existence of a third sex.

Though considered tame in today's language, the book's publication was met with a shocked fury and disbelief and it was subsequently withdrawn at the behest of the British Home Secretary, with all copies seized under the Obscene Publications Act. As with many scandals, the publicity propelled the novel to enormous success and few lesbians have not flicked through it at some point.

The very facts of Hall's personal life – her 'theft' of two men's wives (Mabel Batten and Una Troubridge) and her adoption of masculine dress (smoking jacket, Eton crop and monocle) – exacerbated the public outrage. How dare such a perverted woman make a claim for the moral high ground? There has been much debate about the book's characters and the less than positive light in which Hall portrays lesbianism but, all argument aside, the novel was a brave and committed attempt to increase the consciousness of an Anglo-Saxon world that had previously almost entirely ignored the phenomenon.

On its publication, *The Well Of Loneliness* experienced a rollercoaster of what would today be considered excellent publicity but which, in those days, resulted in Hall and her lover, Troubridge, heading off to France for good.

JULY 1928   *The Well Of Loneliness*, is published in Paris and goes into multiple printings as a result of its popularity.

NOVEMBER 1928   UK court action begins against Hall. Despite a protest action from people as varied and well known as George Bernard Shaw and HG Wells, the book is nevertheless declared obscene and further sales are banned in England.

15 DECEMBER 1928 *The Well of Loneliness* is published in the US, where over 20,000 copies are sold, making it a bestseller.

19 APRIL 1929   In New York City, an appellate court overrules the verdict reached earlier in the year by a lower court that *The Well Of Loneliness* is not obscene. The decision allows yet more sales to occur, thereby garnering Hall's novel its special place in lesbian literary history.

— FORNICATION IN THE US CAPITAL —

Although Washington's sodomy law was repealed back in 1995, there is still a statute (Section 22–1602) that prohibits sexual intercourse between unmarried people. The Fornication Law states that 'if any unmarried man or woman commits fornication in the District, each shall be fined not more than $300 or imprisoned not more than six months or both'.

— NO OSCAR WILDES ALLOWED —

The county commissioners of Rhea County, Tennessee – located about 30 miles from Chattanooga – decided that it was time to take a stand on the same-sex-marriage issue. On 16 March 2004, they voted 8–0 to approve a motion to ask the county's state representatives to introduce legislation that would keep 'homosexuals out of here'. Under the legislation, homosexuals could be charged with 'crimes against nature' and, if convicted, put in prison.

The media quickly descended on the county, which had previously made headlines back in 1925 when high-school teacher John T Scopes was convicted of teaching evolution theory and fined $100. The conviction was later overturned.

The county commissioners realised that there might have been some confusion surrounding the exact wording of the measure, which was rescinded a few days later. It's still doubtful whether there will be signs posted welcoming homos to Rhea County any time soon.

— THE LADIES OF LLANGOLLEN —

Eleanor Butler (1739–1829) and Sarah Ponsonby (1755–1831) were Irish cousins who were sufficiently close to be called 'kissing cousins' – to the extent that they eloped to Wales together in 1778, dressed in men's clothing to evade capture. They set up home in Plas Newydd, in north Wales, where they lived a celebrated and admired life for the next few decades. Idealised by their (mainly heterosexual) peers for the purity of their friendship – which was, however, seen as not sexual – some contemporaries saw fit to refer to them as 'sapphists', suggesting that not everyone believed theirs to be a purely platonic relationship.

— EVERY COUPLE COUNTS —

The 2000 United States Census reported a total of 598,209 same-sex partner households (301,148 gay male families and 297,061 lesbian families). The 2000 Census did not count single gays or lesbians, nor did it count people who were in relationships but not living in the same household.

Here's a list of the states with the highest number of same-sex unmarried-couple households:

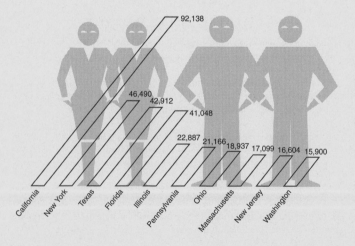

California 92,138
New York 46,490
Texas 42,912
Florida 41,048
Illinois 22,887
Pennsylvania 21,166
Ohio 18,937
Massachusetts 17,099
New Jersey 16,604
Washington 15,900

Now here are ten places in the US (with over 100,000 population) with the highest percentage of same-sex unmarried-partner households:

RANK	US CITY	% OF ALL HOUSEHOLDS
1	San Francisco, CA	2.7
2	Fort Lauderdale, FL	2.1
3	Seattle, WA	1.9
4	Oakland, CA	1.8
5	Berkeley, CA	1.8
6	Atlanta, GA	1.7
7	Minneapolis, MN	1.6
8	Washington, DC	1.5
9	Long Beach, CA	1.4
10	Portland, OR	1.3

— THE GATEWAYS CLUB —

The most famous London lesbian club in post-war Britain, the Gateways Club was originally opened in the 1930s as a meeting place for bohemians and the artistic community, but after World War II the establishment began to play host to increasing numbers of lesbian clientèle. Gina, the proprietor, initially ran the club with her husband, but later with her lesbian lover, Smithy. The bar was featured in the 1968 film *The Killing Of Sister George*, and Dusty Springfield is said to have been a frequent visitor.

— LESBIAN TOP-TEN HEALTH CONCERNS —

1. Breast cancer
2. Depression/anxiety
3. Gynaecological cancer
4. Fitness issues
5. Substance abuse
6. Smoking
7. Alcohol consumption
8. Domestic violence
9. Osteoporosis
10. Heart trouble

— REQUIRED GAY READING: REAL-LIFE STORIES —

AUTOBIOGRAPHIES

AILEY, ALVIN: *Revelations: The Autobiography Of Alvin Ailey* (1995)

ARENAS, REINALDO (Cuban writer): *Before Night Falls: A Memoir* (1993)

BURROUGHS, AUGUSTEN (writer): *Running With Scissors* (2002) and *Dry: A Memoir* (2003)

BEAN, BILLY (ex-baseball outfielder), with Chris Hull: *Going The Other Way: Lessons From A Life In And Out Of Major League Baseball* (2003)

CHAPMAN, GRAHAM (comedian/Monty Pythoner): *A Liar's Autobiography* (1981)

CRISP, QUENTIN (writer/author): *The Naked Civil Servant* (1968)

DOTY, MARK (poet): *Firebird: A Memoir* (1999)

DUBERMAN, MARTIN: *Cures: A Gay Man's Odyssey* (1991)

ISHERWOOD, CHRISTOPHER (writer): *Christopher And His Kind* (1976) and *Diaries: 1939–1960* (1996)

JARMAN, DEREK (artist/filmmaker): *At Your Own Risk: A Saint's Testament* (1992)

KOPAY, DAVE (ex-pro football player): *The Dave Kopay Story* (1977)

LOUGANIS, GREG (Olympic medallist/world champion diver): *Breaking The Surface* (1995)

VON MAHLSDORF, CHARLOTTE: *I Am My Own Woman: The Outlaw Life Of Charlotte Von Mahlsdorf, Berlin's Most Distinguished Transvestite* (1995)

MONETTE, PAUL (writer): *Becoming A Man: Half A Life Story* (1992) and *Borrowed Time: An AIDS Memoir* (1988)

REID, JOHN (aka Andrew Tobias, finance columnist/author): *Best Little Boy In The World* (1973)

SPENDER, STEPHEN (poet): *World With World* (2001)

VIDAL, GORE (writer): *Palimpsest: A Memoir* (1995)

WHITE, MEL: *Stranger At The Gate: To Be Gay And Christian In America* (1994)

BIOGRAPHIES (ALPHABETICAL BY SUBJECT)

WHITE, EDMUND: *Genet: A Biography* (1994)

MANN, WILLIAM J: *Wisecracker: The Life And Times Of William Haines* (1999)

GIBSON, IAN: *Federico Garcia Lorca* (1989)

KAUFMAN, DAVID: *Ridiculous! The Theatrical Life And Times Of Charles Ludlam* (2002)

SHILTS, RANDY: *The Mayor Of Castro Street: The Life And Times Of Harvey Milk* (1988)

STOKES, HENRY SCOTT: *The Life And Death Of Yukio Mishima* (1998)

SOARES, ANDRE: *Beyond Paradise: The Life Of Ramon Novarro* (2002)

ANDERSON, JERVIS: *Bayard Rustin: Troubles I've Seen – A Biography* (1997)

ELLMAN, RICHARD: *Oscar Wilde* (1988)

WINICK, JUDD: *Pedro* [Zamora] *And Me – Friendship, Loss, And What I Learned* (2000)

— AFRICAN TRIBES WITH REPORTED LESBIAN — SEXUAL PRACTICES

Tswana (southern Africa)
Ila (southern Africa)
Naman (southern Africa)
Azande (Sudan)
Ovimbundu (Angola)

— BED-DEATH BOREDOM —

Lesbian Bed Death is a phrase used to describe the inverse relationship between a lesbian couple's frequency of sex and the longevity of their partnership. The term is typically laughed at and rejected, a source of humour often used to wind up mates that have been together for more than a few months. Some believe it to be an inevitable part of any long-term lesbian relationship, with reports suggesting that lesbians have less sex than those of any other sexual orientation. This assertion would, however, be challenged by the numerous sexually successful dyke couples out there.

— BIRDS OF A FEATHER —

In 1977, George and Molly Hunt caused a furore in academic circles and the mass media by their assertion of the existence of lesbian gulls. They had observed girl-on-girl behaviour in seagulls which contradicted the widely held belief that lesbianism was unnatural. However, lesbian swans had been reported as far back as 1885.

— EL MUNDO DE PEDRO ALMODÓVAR —

Pedro Almodóvar is one of Spain's most popular (and prolific) directors, best known for his subversive, campy comedies and melodramas, many of which were inspired by Hollywood films of the 1940s and '50s.

At the age of 17, Almodóvar left his home town, Calzada de Calatrava, and moved to Madrid, where he worked for 12 years as a telephone operator. Consequently, telephones and answering machines figure prominently in his films. In *Law Of Desire*, for example, a lesbian transsexual actress (played by Carmen Maura) is performing Jean Cocteau's one-woman play, *The Human Voice*, in which a woman who has recently split with her lover has a nervous breakdown as she talks to him on the telephone. *Women On The Verge Of A Nervous Breakdown* contains a similar scenario, whereby a distraught actress – played once again by Maura – discovers she is being dumped by her married lover when she hears the message he left on her answering machine.

Almodóvar was living in Madrid in the post-Franco era, a period known as La Movida (one of those terms that's difficult to define but, translated, suggests 'moving forward'), during which Spanish culture and nightlife thrived. At this time he was the lead singer in a cross-dressing punk rock duo, Almodóvar and McNamara, and a comic-book illustrator, and it was then that he started to make 8mm film shorts. His early projects included *Sex Comes, Sex Goes* (1977), in which a guy becomes a woman when his girlfriend decides she likes girls, and *Fuck...Fuck...Fuck Me...Tim* (1978) a feature-length Super 8mm film that tells the tragic story of a poor girl who goes blind at the same time that her guitar-playing blind boyfriend becomes famous.

Almodóvar's films are produced by his brother, Augustin Almodóvar, who usually plays a cameo, along with their mother, Francisca Caballero.

— BLISTERED BEAVER —

Try as you might, stimulating the labia majora will result in nothing more than a touch of carpet burn. The outside lips of the vulva have been described as the least excitable part of female genitalia. The most sensitive erogenous zones are rated in descending order as being the clitoris, the vagina near the clitoris, the inside lips of the vulva (labia minora), inside the vagina and the breasts. Lesbian sex is often more anatomically informed than that between differing genders – after all, women tend to know their own bodies – yet legend has it that many het and bi women are plagued by the erroneous belief similarly held by some blokes that the vulva is something to be twiddled about with like the knobs on the radio!

— LOST IN TRANSLATION —

A quick list of bisexual or gay men portrayed as heterosexuals:

SUBJECT	ACTOR	FILM	YEAR
Alexander the Great	Richard Burton	*Alexander The Great*	1956
Stephen Foster	Don Ameche	*Swanee River*	1939
General Charles Gordon	Charleton Heston	*Khartoum*	1966
Cole Porter	Cary Grant	*Night And Day*	1946
Hans Christian Andersen	Danny Kaye	*Hans Christian Andersen*	1952
TE Lawrence	Peter O'Toole	*Lawrence Of Arabia*	1962
Michelangelo	Charlton Heston	*The Agony And The Ecstasy*	1956
Rudolph Valentino	Anthony Dexter	*Valentino*	1951

— FIRST JAPANESE GAY PRIDE MARCH —

More than 1,200 lesbians, gay men and their supporters amassed in Tokyo for Japan's first lesbian and gay Pride march in August 1994.

— PASSING WOMEN —

Passing women is a term used to describe women, particularly during the 19th century, who chose to dress as men, work for men's wages, court and marry women they loved and even vote. Passing women succeeded in hiding their female identities from most of the world, claiming the economical and political privileges enjoyed by men. There are innumerable reports of women whose gender was discovered only at their deaths or during illness, and it has been suggested that estimates of the numbers of passing women in history have been grossly underestimated.

• Dr Eugene C Perkins was married to another woman for 28 years and was discovered to be female on her death in 1936.

• Dr James Miranda Barry (c1795–1865), the most famous British woman to go to war, rose to become inspector general of army hospitals.

• Murray Hall was a woman who passed as a man for 25 years, becoming an influential politician in the 1880s and 1890s.

All passing women were constantly in danger of exposure. Arrest and incarceration in a jail or an insane asylum were probable and – unless you were wealthy or a person of stature – quite difficult to avoid.

• Mary 'George' Hamilton (1721–?) was an English passing woman who was arrested and prosecuted in 1776, under a clause in the Vagrancy Act, 'for having by false and deceitful practices endeavoured to impose on some of his Majesty's subjects'. She was shown to have deceived several women about her gender, marrying two of them. At the trial, an exhibit of 'vile, wicked and scandalous nature' (probably a dildo) was unearthed in the trunk of the accused and was subsequently produced in evidence of her ability to deceive. Found guilty, Hamilton was publicly whipped in four market towns and imprisoned for six months.

• Ann Marrow was convicted of fraud in 1777 for 'going in man's cloths, and personating a man in marriage with three different women' and 'defrauding them of their money and effects'. She was sentenced to three months in prison and made to stand in the pillory at Charing Cross, London, where she was pelted with stones so severely that she was blinded in both eyes.

The number of cross-dressing women who are generally believed to have had lesbian relations is extensive. The stories of Cora Anderson, Lillie

Hitchcock Coit, Charlie Parkhurst, Jeanne Bonnet, Luisa Matson and Babe Bean have been oft cited in reference to passing women. However, these are but a handful of vast accounts, many revealed in autobiographies later in their lives.

'IF THIS ISN'T LOVE...'
— LONG-TERM GAY MALE COUPLES —

Bruhs Mero (dancer/lyricist) and **Gean Harwood** (pianist, composer, author). Known as the 'The Oldest Gay Couple in America' ....66 years

George Nader (1921–2001, actor) and **Mark Miller** ....55 years

Merce Cunningham (dancer/choreographer) and **John Cage** (1912–92, composer)..54 years

JC Leyendecke (1874–1951, illustrator) and **Charles Beach** (1886–1952)..49 years

William Haines (1900–73, actor/decorator) and **Jimmy Shields**.....47 years

Axel Agil and **Agil Axel** (gay activists, the world's first 'registered couple')...46 years

J Edgar Hoover (1895–1972, FBI director) and **Clyde Tolson** (FBI special agent) ....46 years

Edward Perry Warren (1860–1928, art connoisseur) and **John Marshall** (archaeologist)...44 years

Sir John Gielgud (1904–2000, actor) and **Martin Hensler**.............40 years

Benjamin Britten (1913–76, composer) and **Peter Pears** (tenor).....40 years

Harry Hay (1912–2002, activist) and **John Burnside** (activist) ......39 years

James Ivory (filmmaker) and **Ishmael Merchant** (filmmaker) ....39 years

Raymond Burr (1917–93, actor) **Robert Benevides** (philanthropist)..35 years

Paul Cadmus (1904–99, artist) and **Jon Andersson** ....35 years

WH Auden (1907–73, poet) and **Chester Kalman** ....34 years

Lou Harrison (composer) and **William Colvig**...............................33 years

Ned Rorem (composer) and **James Holmes** ....32 years

Edward Carpenter (1844–1929, writer) and **George Merrill** ....30 years

Christopher Isherwood (1904–86, writer) and **Don Bachardy** (artist)...30 years

James Bridges (1935–93, director) and **Jack Larson** (actor/producer)..30 years

John Schlesinger (1926–2003, director) and **Michael Childers** (photographer) ....30 years

— ENDANGERED ICONS —

FRANCIS FAYE (1911–91)

Faye was a sassy, versatile jazz and blues singer/songwriter who got her start in vaudeville and then became a regular on the nightclub circuit. The very first openly gay female performer, she had a style all of her own, which probably kept her from becoming a mainstream recording or television star. Still, she always maintained a strong gay and lesbian following. Faye made her screen debut in 1937 in *Double Or Nothing*, in which she plays a sister act with Martha Raye, starring alongside Bing Crosby. She returned to the screen 40 years later, playing a madam in Louis Malle's *Pretty Baby* (1977). Her short list of recordings includes a 1956 studio version of *Porgy And Bess* and *Frances Fay: Caught In The Act*, which was recorded live at the Crescendo in Hollywood in 1958. As Faye would say, 'Francis Faye/Gay, gay, gay/Is there another way?'

WAYLAND FLOWERS (1939–88) AND MADAME

Flowers was a talented puppeteer best known as the voice of Madame, a sharp-tongued, potty-mouthed old lady puppet who thought she looked glamorous in her evening gown, tiara and feather boa. Madame was never shy when it came to expressing her opinions about men and sex. She also took pleasure in dishing out the insults and zingers, which she directed towards her guests on her short-lived syndicated talk show *Madame's Place*. Before getting her own show in 1983, Flowers and Madame made frequent appearances on *Laugh-In* and *The Hollywood Squares*.

BEA LILLIE (1894–1989)

Lillie was a Canadian-born comedienne/singer who became a star on both the London and New York stages and made a few films during the late Silent Era and early Golden Era. She married Robert Peel in 1920 and later became Lady Peel when her husband inherited his father's title. Dubbed by *New York Times* critic Brooks Atkinson 'the funniest woman in the world', Lillie entertained the troops during World War II – an act for which she was honoured by General Charles de Gaulle – and then toured in her one-woman show, *An Evening With Beatrice Lillie*. She returned to Broadway in 1958, when she took over for Rosalind Russell in *Auntie Mame*. Lillie's career started to wane in the 1960s, although she did return to the screen as the villainous Mrs Meers in the film musical *Thoroughly Modern Millie*, yet her brand of entertainment was by now considered passé. She started to show signs of Alzheimer's syndrome and suffered a series of strokes, which made her an invalid up until her death at the age of 93.

— THE SAPPHIC STANZA —

Most people know about Sappho and what she's come to represent in lesbian history. While to be sapphic or a sapphist is to be a lesbian, there is an earlier meaning of the word. In its original form, *sapphic* was a term used to describe a classical Greek stanza (used by the poet Sappho) that comprised four unrhymed lines. The first three lines are written in trochaic pentameter, except for the third foot, which is a dactyl, while the fourth line has only two feet: a dactyl and a trochee.

— THE MOTHER OF THE BLUES —

Ma Rainey was born Gertrude Pridgett on 26 April 1886 in Columbus, Georgia, USA. Her parents were both minstrel entertainers and so the move into performing was always a likely one for the young Gertrude. She began her stage career at the age of just 14 with a song-and-dance troupe. In 1902, when she heard her first blues song in St Louis, she was quick to incorporate it into her act, and it wasn't long before *her* blues was *the* blues.

Gertrude married one Will 'Pa' Rainey in 1904, also an entertainer, and they toured the southern USA as Ma And Pa Rainey And Assassinators Of The Blues. However, Ma Rainey was definitely the talent of the act, and she went on to perform solo and is credited for the rise in popularity of blues music in America at the dawn of the 20th century. Today, Ma Rainey is usually known as the Mother of the Blues.

A hard worker, Ma also liked to play hard too, and she wasn't too fussed about whether she played with boys or with girls. She even went as far as to sing about it on 1928's 'Prove It On Me', in which she talks of hanging out exclusively with women, as she did not like men. There are numerous stories – some less reliable than others – of her wild parties, her jealous relationships with the girls in her troupe and the outright way in which she conducted her affairs with women. Ma Rainey might have pioneered the blues, but she was also one of the early pioneers of being out of the closet.

— THE AIDS MEMORIAL QUILT —

The AIDS Memorial Quilt is a memorial to the many people who have died of AIDS-related illnesses. The quilt was conceived in 1985 by gay activist Cleve Jones, who was mourning the loss of his lover of 14 years, Marvin Feldman, to the syndrome. That same year he organised an AIDS march through the streets of San Francisco to the Federal Building, where protestors held up placards bearing the names of their friends, family and partners who had died. The sight of all of the names side by side reminded Jones of a patchwork quilt.

Two years later, Jones and Mike Smith founded the NAMES Project Foundation, which started receiving quilts from around the country. The Memorial Quilt, which comprised 1,920 panels, went on display for the first time on 11 October 1987 at the National Mall during the National March on Washington for Lesbian and Gay Rights. When the Quilt returned in the following year, the number of panels had grown to 8,288.

As the Quilt continued to grow, so did the Names Project, which currently has 21 chapters in the US and 46 affiliates around the world. The Quilt has been displayed in its entirety on five separate occasions – in 1987, 1988, 1989, 1992 and 1996 – and now consists of 5,690 blocks (12-foot squares made of 8 separate panels) for a total of approximately 45,500 individual panels. There are no immediate plans to display the entire Quilt again, although 1,000 new blocks were on display in Washington, DC, on 24–27 June 2004.

The Quilt was nominated for the Nobel Peace Prize in 1989 and is the subject of the 1989 Academy Award-winning feature documentary *Common Threads: Stories From The Quilt*, directed by Rob Epstein and Jeffrey Friedman.

You can now view the panels online at the Names Project website at www.aidsquilt.org. They bear the names of the following bisexual and gay men. The figure on the right is the number of panels on which each name appears.

Alvin Ailey (1931–89, dancer/choreographer) 3

Peter Allen (1944–92, songwriter/entertainer) 8

Howard Ashman (1950–91, lyricist) 9

Roy Cohn (1927–86, attorney) 2

— THE GAME OF FLATS —

From at least the early 1700s, lesbian sex began to
be referred to as 'the game of flats', or just 'flats'.
This term derives in turn from 'flat fucking' and
was presumably arrived at from the perception that
lesbian sex was primarily tribadistic (ie it essentially
simulated heterosexual behaviour). It was
purported in texts of the time that this frightful
practice came to London from the Turks.

— JAZZ-AGE HARLEM SONGS ABOUT LESBIANS —

'It's Dirty But Good' – Bessie Smith
'BD Women Blues' – Lucille Bogan
'Boy In The Boat' – George Hanna
'B-D Woman' – Bessie Smith
'Prove It On Me' – Ma Rainey

— THANKS FOR THE MEMORIES —

In 1986, comedian Bob Hope entertained at the centenary of the Statue of Liberty. President Ronald Reagan and First Lady Nancy Reagan were seated front and centre with French President François Mitterrand and his wife, Danielle. At one point, Bob Hope quipped, 'I just heard that the Statue of Liberty has AIDS, but she doesn't know if she got it from the mouth of the Hudson or the Staten Island Fairy.' Recordings of the event then show the audience's reaction: Ronnie and Nancy are laughing hysterically; President and Mrs Mitterrand are not amused.

On a 1988 *Tonight Show* appearance, Hope used the word *fag* in reference to someone's colourful tie. GLAAD (Gay and Lesbian Alliance Against Defamation) demanded an apology, which they received in the form of a Public Service Announcement featuring the comedian, who also picked up the tab. In the PSA, a tuxedo-clad Hope stands in front of the camera and says, 'I'm proud to live in this great, free country, and I'm proud of our commitment to free speech. And I'm proud of our country's commitment to protecting the rights of its citizens to work and live free from bigotry and violence. That's why I'm amazed to discover that many people die each year in anti-gay attacks and thousands more are left scarred, emotionally and physically. Bigotry has no place in this world, but it happens. Prejudice hurts, kills. Please don't be a part of it.' The commercial aired on New York City's *Gay Cable Network* and *The 10% Show* in Chicago. At the first annual GLAAD Awards, GLAAD recognised Hope for his efforts. View Hope's PSA announcement at www.commercialcloset.org.

— THE CHILDREN'S HOUR —

On 20 November 1934, Lillian Hellman's play *The Children's Hour* opened on Broadway to rave reviews and sell-out audiences. It told the story of two Scottish schoolteachers, Marianne Woods and Jane Pirie, accused of lesbianism by one of their students, and was based on an actual case in 19th-century Scotland. The play was filmed in 1962 as *The Loudest Whisper*, in which the heroine's epiphany that she is, indeed, a lesbian, necessitates (as was the Hollywood tradition of the time with any gay character) that she die (in this case, suicide). In reality, however, the two women in Scotland brought a successful legal action against the woman who had spread the original rumours. The notoriety of the case led the British authorities in the following year (1812) debating the possibility of sex between two women. Their conclusion? Not possible.

— HAPPY ENDINGS —

1952 saw the publication of Claire Morgan's *The Price Of Salt*, one of the first lesbian novels to offer a happy ending, thereby giving hope to millions of lesbians that there would be a joyful ending to their own stories.

Popular culture of the day had a good tradition of swiftly terminating – in an often brutal fashion – any hint of happiness for gay characters. *The Price Of Salt* was a refreshing and welcome change for most women of the time.

'Claire Morgan' more famously published as Patricia Highsmith, author of the Ripley books and *Strangers On A Train*. *The Price Of Salt* has subsequently been republished under the title *Carol*.

— MIDLER ON MARRIAGE —

In February 2004, President Bush received an email allegedly written by Bette Midler regarding his proposed amendment to the Constitution defining marriage as between a man and a woman.

> ...I mean, honestly, Mr President – how many couples do you know who are together for 51 years? I'm sure you agree that this love story provides a wonderful opportunity to teach our children about the true meaning and value of marriage. On the steps of San Francisco City Hall, rose petals and champagne, suits and veils, horns honking and elation in the streets; a celebration of love the likes of which this society has never seen.

Midler said the email was 'beautifully written, heartfelt and impassioned', but she didn't write it.

— GAY AND LESBIAN FILM FESTIVALS —

AUSTRALIA
- **Sydney** – Mardi Gras Film Festival/Queer Screen Ltd • February • queerscreen.com.au

- **Melbourne** – Queer Film Festival • melbournequeerfilm.com

BELGIUM
- **Brussels** – Pink Screens • May • pinkscreens.org

- **Brussels** – Lesbian and Gay Film Festival • January • fglb.org

BRAZIL
- **São Paulo** – MixBrasil – Film and Video Festival of Sexual Diversity • mixbrasil.uol.com.br

- **Rio de Janiero/Brasília** • November/December

CANADA
- **Toronto** – Inside Out Lesbian and Gay Film and Video Festival • May • insideout.on.ca

- **Vancouver** – Out on Screen: Queer Film and Video Festival • August • outonscreen.com

CZECH REPUBLIC
- **Brno/Prague** – Gay and Lesbian Film Festival in Mezipatra • November • mezipatra.cz

DENMARK
- **Copenhagen** – Gay and Lesbian Film Festival • October • cglff.dk

ENGLAND
- **London** – Lesbian and Gay Film Festival • March/April • llgff.org.uk

FINLAND
- **Turku/Helsinki** – Vinokino Lesbian and Gay Film Festival • November tuseta.fi/vinokino

FRANCE
- **Paris** – Gay and Lesbian Film Festival • November • ffglp.net

- **Grenoble** – International Gay and Lesbian Film Festival • April • vuesdenface.free.fr

GERMANY
- **Munich/Berlin/Frankfurt/Cologne** – Verzaubert International Film Festival • verzaubertfilmfest.com

- **Berlin** – Lesbian Film Festival • October • lesbenfilmfestival.de

- **Cologne** – Feminale International Women's Biannual Film Festival • feminale.de

- **Hamburg** – Lesbian and Gay Film Festival • October • lsf-hamburg.de

USA
- **Arizona** – OutFar! International Lesbian and Gay Film Festival • Phoenix • February • outfar.org

- **Atlanta** – Out on Film Gay and Lesbian Film Festival • November • outonfilm.com

- **California** – Outfest: The Los Angeles Gay and Lesbian Film Festival • July • outfest.org

- **California** – San Francisco International Lesbian and Gay Film Festival • June • frameline.org/festival/

- **Chicago** – Reeling Lesbian and Gay International Film Festival • November • reelingfilm festival.org

- **Colorado** – International GLBT Film Festival • Denver • April • denverfilmfestival.com

- **Connecticut** – Gay and Lesbian Film Festival • New Hartford • June • CTGLFF.org

- **Hawaii** – Rainbow Film Festival • Honolulu • May • hglcf.org

- **Indianapolis** – LGBT Film Festival • September • windylgbtfilmfest.com

- **Miami** – Annual Gay and Lesbian Film Festival • April • mglff.com

— GAY AND LESBIAN FILM FESTIVALS (CONT'D) —

- **Miami** – Tampa International Gay and Lesbian Film Festival • October • tiglff.com

- **Michigan** – Reel Pride LGBT Film Festival • Detroit • January • reelpridemichigan.com

- **Missouri** – Gay and Lesbian Film Festival • Kansas City • kcgayfilm.org

- **New York** – NewFest Lesbian, Gay, Lesbian and Transsexual Film Festival • June • newfestival.org

- **North Carolina** – Gay and Lesbian Film Festival • Durham • August • carolinatheatre.org/ncglff

- **Oklahoma** – Out-OK International Film Festival • Oklahoma City/Tulsa • October • out-ok.com

— EDUCATING LESBIANS —

Eminent sex-researcher Alfred C Kinsey's research in the USA during the 1940s revealed some correlation between levels of education and experience of lesbian sex. In a study of women aged 30, the percentage with homosexual experience appeared to be higher with increasing education levels. His findings are outlined below:

Education Level	Homosexual Experience to Orgasm
College	9-10%
No College	17%
Some Grad School	24%

— ANDY WARHOL'S *BLOW JOB* —

In the mid 1960s, pop artist Andy Warhol shifted his attention from painting to filmmaking because he claimed that making movies was easier, because you can just turn the camera on and walk away. Among the many films he produced between 1965 and 1968 is a 36-minute black-and-white silent film entitled *Blow Job* (1963), which consists of a stationary shot of a nameless, handsome young man (his identity is unknown) leaning against a brick wall. The lower part of the man's body (from the waist down) is out of view, but judging from the expression on his face, he seems to be getting a blow job, which goes on for the next 30 minutes or so until the boy – and the film – reach a climax.

— kd lang DISCOGRAPHY —

Year	Album Title	Label
2003	Tony Bennett & kd lang: *Wonderful World*	Sire Records
2001	*Live By Request*	Sire Records
2000	*Invincible Summer*	Sire Records
1997	*Drag*	Sire Records
1995	*All You Can Eat*	Sire Records
1993	*Even Cowgirls Get The Blues*	Sire Records
1992	*Ingénue*	Sire Records
1989	*Absolute Torch And Twang*	Sire Records
1988	*Shadowland*	Sire Records
1987	*Angel With A Lariat*	Sire Records
1984	*A Truly Western Experience*	Bumstead Records

— FIRST LESBIAN MAGAZINE —

In Los Angeles in June 1947, 'Lisa Ben' penned the very first lesbian newsletter, *Vice Versa*. The editor's name was an anagram for the obvious and a pseudonym for Edith Eyde. The magazine, billed as 'America's gayest magazine', featured arts reviews and poetry as well as a positive outlook toward lesbianism. Eyde mailed it to 12 recipients.

— GAY/STRAIGHT SONGWRITING TEAMS —

And who said we can't all get along? Here are four pairs of gay/straight songwriters. The gay guy's name is in capitals.

Sir William S Gilbert(1836–1911, playwright/lyricist) and SIR ARTHUR SULLIVAN (1842–1900, composer) – Celebrated British duo who gained an international reputation for their comic operettas, including *HMS Pinafore* (1878), *The Pirates Of Penzance* (1879) and *The Mikado* (1885). As for their personal relationship, the duo were usually at odds with one another; Gilbert reportedly severed ties with Sullivan over a financial matter sparked by the purchase of a $500 carpet for their theatre by their producer, Richard D'Oyly Carte. Gilbert refused to pay his third of the cost, and when Sullivan sided with D'Oyly Carte, Gilbert wrote his partner a note stating, 'The time for putting an end to our collaboration has arrived.'

Richard Rodgers (1902–79, composer) and LORENZ HART (1895–1943, lyricist) – Rodgers and Hart teamed up in 1919 and started out writing songs for amateur productions. Their first big success was *The Garrick Gaieties* (1925), a revue performed as a fundraiser for the Theatre Guild featuring the company's younger performers (which included future acting gurus Lee Strasberg, Sanford Meisner and, later in its run, a young Rosalind Russell). For the next 18 years, Rodgers and Hart were responsible for a string of Broadway hits, including *On Your Toes* (1936), *Babes In Arms* (1937), *The Boys From Syracuse* (1938) and *Pal Joey* (1940). They also wrote scores for several films, including *Love Me Tonight* (1932, starring Maurice Chevalier) and *Hallelujah, I'm A Bum* (1933, starring Al Jolson). Their catalogue of classic songs includes 'My Funny Valentine', 'Falling In Love With Love' and 'Sing For Your Supper'. Their collaboration ended in the early 1940s due to the alcoholism of Hart, who literally drank himself into a coma. He died in 1943 at the age of 48.

John Kander (born 1927, composer) and FRED EBB (born 1933, lyricist) – One of Broadway's most successful teams, Kander and Ebb's career spans over four decades, beginning with *Flora, The Red Menace* (1965), starring a young Liza Minnelli, who later appeared in the screen version of the songwriting duo's *Cabaret*, and on stage and screen in *The Act* (1977) and *The Rink* (1984). Their long list of Broadway musicals includes *Zorba* (1968), *Chicago* (1975), *Woman Of The Year* (1981) and *Kiss Of The Spider Woman* (1993).

HOWARD ASHMAN (1950–91, lyricist) and Alan Mencken (born 1949, composer) – The Oscar-wining songwriting team responsible for the original scores to Disney's *The Little Mermaid* (1989) and *Beauty And The Beast* (1991), as well as songs for *Aladdin* (1992), Ashman and Mencken first teamed up in 1982 on the stage musical *Little Shop Of Horrors*, which was adapted for the screen in 1986. Ashman died due to AIDS in 1991. His partner, Bill Lauch, accepted the Oscar he was awarded posthumously for the song 'Beauty And The Beast' in 1992.

— LAMBDA LITERARY AWARDS —

A prestigious American institution established in 1989 and recognising and honouring the best in lesbian, gay, bisexual and transgender literature, the Lambda Awards are organised by the *Lambda Book Report*, a bi-monthly non-fiction journal that reviews gay and lesbian books and authors. The annually presented trophy is awarded to the author of the winning book, generally published in the preceding year. In 2004, nominations were received in 20 categories:

- Children/Young Adult
- LGBT Humour
- LGBT Drama
- LGBT Erotica
- Science Fiction/Fantasy/Horror
- Spirituality
- Visual Arts
- LGBT Romance
- LGBT Fiction Anthology
- LGBT Non-Fiction Anthology
- Gay Men's Mystery
- Lesbian Mystery
- LGBT Biography
- LGBT Memoir/Autobiography
- Lesbian Poetry
- Gay Men's Poetry
- Transgender
- LGBT Studies
- Gay Men's Fiction
- Lesbian Fiction

The winners are chosen by a panel of 74 judges, who are selected to represent the diverse gay/lesbian/bisexual/transgender literary community.

— LAMBDA LITERARY AWARDS (CONT'D) —

LAMBDA LITERARY AWARD WINNERS – LESBIAN FICTION

LAMBDA	TITLE	AUTHOR	PUBLISHER
16th	*Southland*	Nina Revoyr	Akashic Books
15th	*Fingersmith*	Sarah Waters	Riverhead Books
14th	*Days Of Awe*	Achy Obejas	Ballantine
13th	*Valencia*	Michelle Tea	Seal Press
12th	*Tipping The Velvet*	Sarah Waters	Riverhead Books
11th	*Cavedweller*	Dorothy Allison	Dutton
10th	*Beyond The Pale*	Elana Dykewomon	Press Gang
9th	*Memory Mambo*	Achy Obejas	Cleis
8th	*Autobiography Of A Family Photo*	Jacqueline Woodson	Dutton
7th	*Gifts Of The Body*	Rebecca Brown	HarperCollins
6th	*Written On The Body*	Jeanette Winterson	Alfred A Knopf
5th	*Running Fiercely Toward A High Thin Sound*	Judith Katz	Firebrand Books
4th (tie)	*Revolution Of Little Girls*	Blanche McCrary Boyd	Alfred A Knopf
	Gilda Stories	Jewelle Gomez	Firebrand Books
3rd	*Out Of Time*	Paula Martinac	Seal Press
2nd	*The Bar Stories*	Nisa Donnelly	Firebrand Books
1st	*Trash*	Dorothy Allison	Firebrand Books

— WE INTERRUPT THIS NEWSCAST… —

On 11 December 1973, the live broadcast of the 6:30pm edition of the *CBS Evening News*, hosted by Walter Cronkite, was interrupted when gay activist Mark Segal stepped in front of the camera, held up a handmade sign reading 'GAYS PROTEST CBS PREJUDICE' and shouted, 'Gay people are protesting CBS's policies!' The picture went to black for a few seconds as the stage manager pulled Segal away. A confused Cronkite, who was in the middle of a story about Secretary of State Henry Kissinger, said, 'Well, a rather interesting development in the studio here – a protest demonstration right in the middle of the CBS News Studio.'

Segal later identified himself as a member of 'The Gay Raiders', who were protesting the network's lack of coverage of various gay-rights bills that were currently being voted on around the country. At his trial, Segal had the chance to explain this to Cronkite. The anchorman must have been listening because several months later Cronkite devoted a segment of the news to the gay rights issue.

This was not Segal's first on-air protest (which he referred to collectively as 'zaps'). Previously, he had interrupted a local newscast in Philadelphia, tapings of *The Mike Douglas Show* and *The Tonight Show* (by handcuffing himself to Johnny Carson's desk) and a live broadcast of NBC's *Today* show.

— FRENCH KISSING —

Françoise Marie Antoinette Joseph Saucerotte ('Raucourt') was a French *tragédienne* and actress who lived from 1756 to 1815. The daughter of a third-rate actor, she rose to become a well-known female star of the Comédie Française who enchanted the nobility and dazzled the masses. She was beautiful, expressive and intelligent with a superb voice, the combination of which guaranteed her success upon the stage and beyond. Protected by Marie Antoinette and admired by Napoleon Bonaparte, she 'married' the German female opera singer Jeanne-Françoise Marie Souck (or Sourques) with none of the usual repercussions of derision or punishment.

According to the tabloids of her day, Raucourt headed up the lesbian Sect of Anandrynes, a lesbian secret society founded in 1770 by Thérèse de Fleury. Whatever scandal followed her (and there were a few), she was the pre-eminent lesbian of her day, with what was – for a lesbian – an uncharacteristically massive public following. When she died, the nation mourned and her funeral saw a 15,000-strong crowd in attendance. She is buried in Père Lachaise Cemetery in Paris.

— KINGS WHO WERE ALSO QUEENS —

ALEXANDER THE GREAT (356–323BC) – Macedonian king and world conqueror who was in love with his companion, a cavalry commander name Hephastion (the nature of their relationship is debated by scholars). When Hephastion died of typhus in 325BC, a distraught Alexander apparently cremated his body on a 200-foot pyre and died soon afterwards.

KING AL-MUTAMID (ABBAD III) (1040–95) – Romantic 11th-century Arabian poet and ruler of Seville who had a love affair with poet Ibn'Ammar.

KING ASHURBANIPAL (RULED 668–627BC) – Assyrian ruler who liked to cross-dress. He left behind an extensive library, comprising 22,000 clay tablets, which has served as a primary source of information about Babylonian and Assyrian literature.

KING CONRADIN HOHENSTAUFEN OF SUEDE (RULED 1252–68) – The son of Bavarian king Conrad IV and ruler of Jerusalem and Sicily. He was captured by Charles I, who was given Sicily and Naples by Pope Clement IV in exchange for Conradin, who was beheaded in Market Square in Naples. His lover, Frederick I, Margrave of Baden, chose to be executed with him. The couple were buried together in the church of the monastery of Santa Maria del Carmine in Naples.

EDWARD II (1284–1327) – English king whose father, Edward I, disapproved of his relationship with close friend Piers Gavaston, who was exiled, only to return when Edward II assumed the throne. When Edward II was overthrown by his political enemies, the King was secretly put to death, and Gavaston was also murdered. Legend has it that Edward was punished for his homosexuality by having a red-hot poker stuck up his rear end.

KING ENRIQUE IV OF CASTILE (1425–74) – Homosexual Spanish king whose nickname was 'El Impotent'. His daughter was denied the throne because the nobility didn't believe that Enrique was her father.

KING FREDERICK II (THE GREAT) (1712–86) – At the age of 18, Frederick tried to run away with his lover, an officer named Hans von Katte. They were caught and Frederick's father sentenced von Katte to death.

KING GUSTAV III OF SWEDEN (1746–92) – Ruling during the age of Enlightenment, King Gustav was a dramatist and a patron of the arts. His death by an assassin's bullet at a masquerade ball was the inspiration for Giuseppe Verdi's 1859 opera *Un ballo in maschera* (*A Masked Ball*).

KING HENRI III OF FRANCE (1551–89) – Transvestite king who enjoyed the company of his young lovers, whom he called his *mignons* (darlings).

KING JAMES I (1566–1625) – King of England and Scotland who had several lovers, including a Scottish boy named Robert Carr and George Villiers, who later became Duke of Buckingham.

KING JEAN II LE BON OF FRANCE (1319–64) – Bisexual king whose lover, Charles de la Cerda, was murdered by French barons because he was given too much power.

KING JUAN II OF CASTILE (1405–54) – Spanish king forced by his wife to execute his lover, administrator and diplomat Alvaro de Luna.

KING LOUIS XIII OF FRANCE (1610–43) – Married a Spanish princess in 1615 but didn't consummate his marriage until 1619.

KING LUDWIG II OF BAVARIA (1845–86) – Nicknamed 'Ludwig the Mad', Ludwig was a great patron of the arts who focused most of his time (and money) on building himself castles and palaces. The eccentric monarch was declared insane and drowned mysteriously a few days later.

— BORN OR MADE? —

In 1641, Thomas Bartholin revised his father's *Institutiones Anatomicae*, the most influential European anatomy text of the century, to provide authoritative support for the theory that an enlarged clitoris is the cause of lesbian desire.

By 1760, Swiss physician Dr Tissot's *Onanisme* supported this then-widely held belief. Tissot considered that the condition was disturbingly common and aligned it to hermaphroditism. Tissot's work was widely translated and republished, thereby cementing the belief of a large clitoris being a biological determinant for lesbianism. It would later support the theories of the early sexologists that homosexuals could help their sexuality as little as heterosexuals.

— HOMOSEXUALITY IN FASCIST ITALY —

Homosexuality was legalised in Italy under the first penal code, adopted in 1889. Thirty-three years later, members of Benito Mussolini's fascist government tried to revive Italy's sodomy law, but *Il Duce* himself opposed the proposal because it was only degenerate foreigners, not virile Italian men, who practised homosexuality. He also thought an anti-sodomy law would keep away tourists, who were vital to the economy, and would result in sensationalistic public trials that could tarnish the good name of Italy.

Although there was no mention of homosexuality in the Italian penal code, the persecution and confinement of homosexuals was justified under the law on the basis of their 'behaviour contrary to the dispositions of the regime', 'crimes against the race' and 'attacks on the ethics and integrity of the people'. Homosexuals, who were commonly referred to as 'subversives' and 'political offenders' of the states, were arrested and quietly exiled to neighbouring islands, such as Sardinia and Ventotene, where they served two- to five-year sentences.

— '80s AND '90s LESBIAN TV CHARACTERS —

PROGRAMME	TYPE	NETWORK	CHARACTER	ACTRESS
Brookside 1982–present	Serial drama	C4	Lindsay Corkhill Beth Jordache Shelley Bowers	Claire Sweeney Anna Friel Alexandra Westcourt
Tenko 1981–84	POW drama	BBC	Nellie Keene	Jeananne Crowley
Mapp & Lucia 1985–86	Comedy	C4	'Quaint' Irene Coles	Cecily Hobbs
Hill Street Blues 1981–87	Police drama	NBC	Officer Kate McBride	Linsday Crouse
Women In Prison 1987–88	Prison sitcom	Fox	Bonnie Harper	Antoinette Byron

Programme	Type	Network	Character	Actress
HeartBeat 1988	Medical drama	ABC	Marilyn McGrath Patti	Gail Strickland Gine Hecht
LA Law 1986–94	Lawyer drama	NBC	Cara Jean ('CJ') Lamb	Amanda Donohue
Pacific Drive 1995–97	Serial drama	9NA	Zoe Marshall Margeaux Hayes Dior Shelby Kay West Sondra Westwood Gemma Patterson	Libby Tanner Virginia Hayes Clodagh Crowe Brigid Kelly Helen Dallimore Katherine Lee
Playing The Field 1997–99	Sports drama	BBC1	Angie Gabi	Tracy Whitwell Saira Todd
Bad Girls 1999–present	Prison drama	ITV	Denny Blood Michelle 'Shell' Doeckly Nikki Wade Helen Stewart Selena Geeson Kris Yates	Alicia Eyo Debra Stephenson Mandana Jones Simone Lahbib Charlotte Lucas Jennifer Ness

FIRST USE OF THE WORD 'HOMOSEXUAL'
— ON RADIO AND FILM —

In November 1953, the historian and philosopher Dr Jacob Bronowski used the word *homosexual* on BBC radio programme *Behind the News*. While the term had been in common use for half a century prior to this, this was significant in that it was the first documented case of its use in an English broadcast medium.

However, it wasn't until December 1961 that the term was used in a movie. Again, it was the British media that pioneered its use, in a film titled *Victim*. The release of the film in the USA, however, was met with a denial of its Motion Picture Code Seal of Approval as a result of its use of the term.

— THE COLOUR OF SEX —

In 1950, the Mattachine Society came into being in the USA and it has, since then, been a well-documented early start to organised gay politics. Less well known, perhaps, is another group that formed in June 1950, also in the USA. The Knights of the Clock was formed by black and white men and women and its focus was interracial relationships, although its scope was to provide support for any interracial couples, whether gay, lesbian or straight.

— SODOMY LAWS —

Male homosexuality is illegal in the following countries under current sodomy laws:

Country	Maximum prison sentence
Algeria	3 years + fine
Bangladesh	Life
Bhutan	Life
Botswana	7 years
Brunei	10 years
Burman/Myanmar	10 years + fine
Cameroon	5 years + fine
Cook Islands	14 years
Cuba	1 year
Ethiopia	3 years
Fiji Islands	14 years
Gambia	14 years
Guinea	3 years
Guyana	Life
India	Life
Jamaica	10 years + hard labour
Kenya	14 years
Kiribati	14 years
Libya	5 years
Mauritius	5 years
Morocco	3 years + fine
Mozambique	3 years/hard labour
Nicaragua	3 years
Saint Lucia	25 years
Senegal	5 years + fine
Somalia	3 years
Tanzania	14 years

Togo ....3 years
Trinidad and Tobago ....10 years
Tunisia..3 years
Zambia...14 years
Zimbabwe ....3 years

Countries in which homosexuality is punishable by death:

Afghanistan
Mauritania
Nigeria
Sudan
Uganda

— UK'S FIRST QUEER MAYOR —

On 13 November 1985, the Manchester politician Margaret Roff became the United Kingdom's first openly lesbian (or gay) mayor.

— THE FIRST GAY ACTIVISTS —

HEINRICH HÖSSLLI (1794–1864)
Hösslli was a Swiss milliner whose interest in the topic of same-sex love was sparked by his son's homosexuality and the execution of a Bern man who murdered his young lover out of despair. Believing that the Swiss sodomy laws were unjust, Hösslli encouraged popular Swiss-German writer Heinrich Zschokke to address the subject. Hösslli didn't agree with Zschokke's conclusion that Greek male love is an aberration, so he put pen to paper and wrote *Eros: über die Männerliebe* (*Eros: On The Love Of Man*), which begins with a question once posed by Benjamin Franklin: 'Have you recently noticed a flaw in the legislation of your fatherland, on account of which it would be advisable to ask the legislative power for an amendment?'

KARL HEINRICH ULRICHS (1825–95)
A German author and advocate of homosexual rights, Karl Ulrichs believed that homosexuality was the result of an abnormal development of the brain, affecting the direction of the sex drive. In 1862, he chose the term *Urning* (derived from the Aphrodite Urania, the God of Heavenly) for individuals who have a male body but feel a sexual love for men and an aversion to women.

— THE FIRST GAY ACTIVISTS (CONT'D) —

JOHN ADDINGTON SYMONDS (1840–93)
Symonds was an English cultural historian and author who privately published *A Problem In Greek Ethics*, a study of homosexuality in ancient Greece. Symonds advocated the repeal of Great Britain's sodomy laws, particularly after the repeal of such laws in France and Italy had caused no negative effects on the morality of its people. On his death, Symonds gave a sealed copy of his memoirs detailing his homosexual life to his executor, who passed it on to the British Library with instructions prohibiting their publication for 50 years. Symonds's memoirs finally landed on bookstore shelves in 1984.

KAROLY MARIA KERTBENY (1824–82)
Kertbeny was a Hungarian doctor who in 1869 wrote a letter to the Minister of Justice protesting the criminalisation of sodomy in the North German Confederation. He is credited for coining the term *homosexualität* (homosexuality).

— POSITIVE PERFORMANCE —

Positive representation of lesbians by mainstream female actors has featured in modern-day popular flicks.

- Brooke Shields plays Janine Nielssen alongside Cherry Jones as Sandy Cataldi in *What Makes A Family*, a 2004 TV-movie based on a true story that recounts a gay woman's struggle to win custody of her daughter after her partner passes away.

- Sharon Stone teams with Ellen DeGeneres to portray a loving couple eager to experience parenthood in the 2000 film *If These Walls Could Talk 2*. In the same movie, Vanessa Redgrave won an Emmy for her performance as an elderly woman 'widowed' when her companion of 50 years dies.

- Meryl Streep shines as Clarissa Vaughan, a present-day version of Virginia Woolf's Mrs Dalloway, in the Academy Award-winning masterpiece *The Hours* (2003).

Lesbians depicted in such a 'normal' and positive light represent a trend toward TV images of gays and lesbians in modern cinematography.

LAMBDA LITERARY AWARD WINNERS:
— LESBIAN MYSTERY —

Year	Title	Author	Publisher
2003	*Damn Straight*	Elizabeth Sims	Alyson Publications
2002 (tie)	*Good Bad Woman*	Elizabeth Woodcraft	Kensington Publishing
	Immaculate Midnight	Ellen Hart	St Martin's Press
2001	*The Merchant Of Venus*	Ellen Hart	St Martin's Press
2000	*Mommy Deadest*	Jean Marcy	New Victoria
1999	*Hunting The Witch*	Ellen Hart	St Martin's Press
1998 (tie)	*Blue Place*	Nicola Griffith	Avon
	Shaman's Moon	Sarah Dreher	New Victoria
1997	*Father Forgive Me*	Randye Lordon	Avon
1996	*Robber's Wine*	Ellen Hart	Seal Press
1995	*Intersection Of Law And Desire*	JM Redmann	WW Norton
1994	*Small Sacrifice*	Ellen Hart	Seal Press
1993	*Divine Victim*	Mary Wings	Dutton
1992 (tie)	*Two Bit Tango*	Elizabeth Pincus	Spinsters Book Co
	Crazy For Loving	Jaye Maiman	Naiad Press
1991	*Murder By Tradition*	Katherine V Forrest	Naiad Press
1990 (tie)	*Gaudi Afternoon*	Barbara Wilson	Seal Press
	Ninth Life	Lauren Wright Douglas	Naiad Press
1989	*The Beverly Malibu*	Katherine V Forrest	Naiad Press
1988	*Skiptrace*	Antoinette Azolakov	Banned Books

— YOUR GAY TICK-IT-OFF FILM LIST —

Film	Seen?
The Adventures Of Priscilla, Queen Of The Desert	
Angels In America	
Another Country	
Bent	
Beautiful Thing	
The Boys In The Band	
La Cage Aux Folles	
Caravaggio	
The Celluloid Closet	
The Crying Game	
Death In Venice	
The Fourth Man	
Fox And His Friends	
The Gay Deceivers	
Get Real	
Gods And Monsters	
Jeffrey	
Kiss Of The Spider Woman	
The Law Of Desire	
The Leather Boys	
Longtime Companion	
Looking For Langston	
Macho Dancer	
Making Love	
A Man Of No Importance	
Maurice	
My Beautiful Launderette	

Film	Seen?
Parting Glances	
Philadelphia	
Prick Up Your Ears	
Priest	
Savage Nights	
Silverlake: The View From Here	
Strawberry And Chocolate	
The Sum Of Us	
Taxi Zum Klo	
Threesome	
Victim	
Victor/Victoria	
Wild Reeds	

— FIRST OSCAR NOMINATION FOR PORTRAYING — A LESBIAN

In 1985, Vanessa Redgrave was nominated for Best Actress for her portrayal of half of a Boston Marriage in the film of Henry James's *The Bostonians*. She thus became the first woman to be nominated for playing a lesbian role.

— MULTI-RACE, MULTI-SEX —

South Africa had its first lesbian and gay Pride march in October 1990. Held in Johannesburg, the event attracted around 800 men and women, both black and white, many of whom were anti-apartheid activists rather than homosexual. The organisers handed out brown paper bags for marchers to wear if they wished to remain anonymous. Unlike many previous marches in apartheid-era South Africa (apartheid was only formally dismantled with the 1995 elections), this one went off relatively peacefully and with the support of the police.

— YOUR LESBIAN TICK-IT-OFF FILM LIST —

FILM	SEEN?
Eight Women	
All Over Me	
Aimee And Jaguar	
Antonia's Line	
Better Than Chocolate	
Bound	
Boys Don't Cry	
But I'm A Cheerleader	
The Children's Hour	
Costa Brava	
Desert Hearts	
Entre Nous	
French Twist	
Gia	
Girls Life	
High Art	
I've Heard The Mermaids Singing	
Je Tu Il Elle	
Love And Other Catastrophes	
Mädchen In Uniform	
Maid Of Honour	
Persona	
Personal Best	
Pourquoi Pas Moi?	
Queen Christina	
Salmonberries	
She Must Be Seeing Things	
Strangers In Good Company	

Film	Seen?
Therese And Isabelle	
Three Of Hearts	
Treasured Past	
When Night Is Falling	

— THE GAY GIRLS' RIDING CLUB —

In the early 1960s, a group of gay men in Los Angeles, most of whom worked in the entertainment industry, went horseback riding in Santa Monica every Sunday morning, followed by brunch at their favourite bar, the Brownstone. One day they decided to pool their talents and spend their Sunday afternoons making a film, which turned out to be a silent parody of the 1960 Greek film *Never On Sunday*, appropriately titled *Always On Sunday*. The film was a hit with the patrons of the Brownstone (where it was shot), so the group – calling themselves The Gay Girls' Riding Club – followed it up in 1962 with *A Roman Springs At Mrs Stone* and *What Really Happened To Baby Jane* in the following year.

The Gay Girls' Riding Club's films were screened in bars around the city and at GGRC-sponsored parties, which often featured live entertainment (their annual Hallowe'en party was the social event of the year). Their final and most ambitious project was their 1972 all-drag send-up of *All About Eve*, entitled *All About Alice*, which also included bits of *Gone With The Wind* and *Strait-Jacket* and a sequence set in 'Ann Miller's Tap Room', where a drag queen imitating you-know-who does a little toe-tapping as she serves her customers.

Among the talented members of the GGRC was Jim Crabe, who become one of Hollywood's leading cameramen, with a long list of television and film credits that includes *Rocky* (1979), *The China Syndrome* (1979) and *The Karate Kid* (1984).

QUEER FACTS

— THE HAYS CODE —

In the early days of cinema, following the hedonistic 1920s, the Motion Picture Producers and Distributors of America (MPPDA) introduced a code of movie ethics aimed at discouraging filmmakers from including frank depictions of sex and sexuality. It was this code that clamped down on the depiction and representation of gay or lesbian characters, relationships or plots in film and which gave rise to a whole generation of movies that hinted at, inferred or suggested gay thematic content until the 1960s allowed a more frank portrayal of such matters. Important to the extent to which it shaped gay and lesbian filmic depiction, here is a brief history of the Hays Code:

- The code was introduced as a self-regulatory code on 1 April 1930 and was soon referred to as 'the Hays Code' after the head of the MPPDA, former Republican National Committee chairman Will H Hays.

- From 1 July 1934, Hollywood eliminated the discretionary element by making adherence to the Code compulsory. Among its provisions:

  - 'Pictures shall not infer that low forms of sex relationships are the accepted or common thing';

  - 'Sex perversion or any inference to it is forbidden on the screen'.

- On 3 October 1961, the MPPDA announced a revision of its production code: 'In keeping with the culture, the mores and the values of our time, homosexuality and other sexual aberrations may now be treated with care, discretion and restraint.' The MPPDA later amended the revision to specify that 'sexual aberration' may be 'suggested but not actually spelled out'.

- Early films to exploit the demise of the code include *Walk On The Wild Side*, *Advise And Consent* and *The Children's Hour*.

— LESBOS DWELLER! —

Written in 520BC, a poem by the Greek poet Anacreon in which he addresses a 'girl from Lesbos' who spurns him and 'gapes at another girl' instead is perhaps the earliest documented use of the word 'Lesbos' in a context suggestive of sexual orientation instead of merely geographical origin. It is merely suggestive, however, and it was only in the Middle Ages that anything more explicit appeared.

— CANDLE POWER —

While today we all know about the different dildos available
(and probably the pros and cons of each), this wasn't always
the case. Dildos have been around in some form for almost
as long as peoplekind, but fashioning them was often very
much a matter of improvisation. Stone was naturally a good
choice but required some refitting work before use;
vegetables such as carrots and marrows offered much more
immediate gratification; and, as many a convent lass would
know, candles have always been a popular option – even
to the extent that knowing poems have been penned in
salutation thereof. In the words of Sir John Suckling,
Cavalier poet:

> 'There is a thing which in the light
> Is seldom used; but in the night
> It serves the female maiden crew
> The ladies and the good-wives too:
> They use to take it in their hand,
> And then it will uprightly stand;
> And to a hole they it apply
> Where by its goodwill it would die;
> It spends, goes out, and still within
> It leaves its moisture thick and thin.'

— GAY HISTORY ON FILM —

Here's a list of documentaries that chronicle the social and political struggles of gay men and lesbians:

BALLOT MEASURE 9 (DIR HEATHER MACDONALD, 1995)
In 1992, Oregon voters considered an anti-gay measure proposed by a conservative group, the Oregon Citizens' Alliance, that would have revoked laws protecting gays and lesbians. Director MacDonald examines the issue from both sides and, in the process, exposes the hatred that fuelled the state-wide campaign, led by the Alliance and the religious right.

BEFORE STONEWALL (DIRS GRETA SCHILLER AND ROBERT ROSENBERG, 1984)
The history of the US gay-rights movement from the 1920s through the 1960s is recounted here through a blend of archival footage and interviews with the gay men and lesbians who were there. A sequel, *After Stonewall* – directed by John Scagliotti, Janet Baus and Dan Hunt – continues the history of the gay-rights movement from Stonewall through to the present day.

COMING OUT UNDER FIRE (DIR ARTHUR DONG, 1994)
This timely documentary on the US military's policies toward homosexuals during World War II features first-hand accounts from the men and women who served. The film is based on the book *Coming Out Under Fire: The History Of Gay Men And Women In World War II* by Allan Berube, who co-wrote the script with Dong, and is narrated by Salome Jens.

THE LIFE AND TIMES OF HARVEY MILK (DIR ROB EPSTEIN AND RICHARD SCHMIECHEN, 1984)
This Academy Award-winning film focuses on the political career and tragic death of San Francisco city councilman Harvey Milk, who was gunned down, along with Mayor George Moscone, by councilman Dan White on 22 November 1978. Narrated by Harvey Fierstein.

PARAGRAPH 175 (DIRS ROB EPSTEIN AND JEFFREY FRIEDMAN, 2000)
Holocaust survivors imprisoned under Germany's anti-gay statute, Paragraph 175, recount their experiences in concentration camps and life in post-war Germany in this moving documentary, narrated by Rupert Everett.

— IT'S FUN TO STAY AT THE YMCA! —

In the spring of 1919, a scandal erupted in Newport, Rhode Island, home to 15,000–20,000 men and boys stationed at the Newport Naval Training Station during World War I. The Station's upper brass had received word that the servicemen who were forced to live at the local YMCA due to overcrowding in the barracks were being 'serviced' for a price by the local hustlers. The Navy therefore asked sailors as young as 16 years old to do their part for Uncle Sam and infiltrate the local homosexual prostitution ring. Their testimony was then used as evidence to court-martial the sailors who got caught.

However, when word got out that the Navy had paid sailors as decoys to perform 'immoral acts' for the purpose of collecting evidence, a Senate subcommittee investigated the matter and reprimanded the commanding officers, among them the former Assistant Secretary of the Navy, Franklin D Roosevelt, whose actions were deemed 'unfortunate', 'ill-advised' and 'reprehensible'. According to a 20 July 1921 *New York Times* article, Roosevelt denied that he directly supervised the operation. As for the Navy's 'hustler brigade', the committee recognised that their assignment 'was practically forced' on them by the senior officers and that, because 'of their patriotism... [they] had responded to the call of the country to defend their flag and their homes'.

A CHRONOLOGY OF 'GAY-THEMED'
— PLAYS AND MUSICALS —

1922   *Saul* (André Gide)

1925   *The Prisoners Of War* (JR Ackerly)

1927   *The Drag* (Mae West)

1933   *Design For Living* (Noël Coward)
        The Green Bay Tree (Mordaunt Shairp)

1936   *The Audience* (Federico Garcia Lorca)

1938   *Oscar Wilde* (Leslie and Sewell Stokes)

1953   *South* (Julien Green)
        Tea And Sympathy (Robert Anderson)

1954   *The Immoralist* (Ruth and Augustus Goetz)

1958   *Suddenly Last Summer* (Tennessee Williams)

1959   *A Taste Of Honey* (Sheila Delaney)

1966   *Loot* (Joe Orton)

1967   *Queen's Collide* (Charles Ludlam)
        Staircase (Charles Dyer)

1969   *Fortune And Men's Eyes* (John Herbert)

1968   *The Boys In The Band* (Mart Crowley)

1970   *Lemon Sky* (Lanford Wilson)
        Small Craft Warnings (Tennessee Williams)

1972   *Street Theater* (Doric Wilson)

1974   *The Ritz* (Terrence McNally)

1975   *PS Your Cat Is Dead* (James Kirkwood)

1977   *Gemini* (Albert Innaurato)
        The Shadow Box (Michael Cristofer)

1978   *Fifth Of July* (Lanford Wilson)

1979   *Bent* (Martin Sherman)

1982   *Execution Of Justice* (Emily Mann)
        The Fairy Garden (Harry Kondoleon)
        Torch Song Trilogy (Harvey Fierstein)

1983	*La Cage Aux Folles* (book by Harvey Fierstein; music and lyrics by Jerry Herman)
1985	*As Is* (William M Hoffman) *The Lisbon Traviata* (Terrence McNally) *Vampire Lesbians Of Sodom* (Charles Busch)
1986	*Jerker, Or The Helping Hand* (Robert Chesley) *Life Of The Party* (Doug Holsclaw) *Night Sweat* (Robert Chesley) *The Normal Heart* (Larry Kramer) *Remedial English* (Evan Smith)
1987	*Breaking The Code* (Hugh Whitemore) *Mean Tears* (Peter Gill) *Safe Sex* (Harvey Fierstein)
1988	*Just Say No* (Larry Kramer) *M Butterfly* (David Henry Hwang) *A Poster Of The Cosmos* (Lanford Wilson)
1992	*Angels In America* (Tony Kushner) *The Destiny Of Me* (Larry Kramer) *Falsettos* (book by James Lapine and William Finn; music and lyrics by William Finn) *Jeffrey* (Paul Rudnick) *Kiss Of The Spider Woman* (book by Terrence McNally; music by John Kander; lyrics by Fred Ebb)
1993	*The Queen Of Angels* (James Carroll Picket)
1994	*Love! Valour! Compassion!* (Terrence McNally)
2003	*Take Me Out* (Richard Greenberg)

— COINING THE TERM 'HOMOSEXUAL' —

In the late 1860s, Karoly Maria Kertbeny, a Hungarian-German translator and bibliographer, began to use the terms *homosexual* and *heterosexual*, derived from *Homo* (the Greek for 'same') and *sexualis* (medieval Latin for 'sexual'). The term was further derived from the French use of the terms *unisexuel* and *bisexuel*, used in reference to botanical studies in the 1790s.

— LESBIAN BOOK PUBLISHERS —

While most mainstream book publishers today don't shy away from publishing gay and lesbian books, some publishers have a long history of publishing almost nothing else (although many often publish women's material in addition to the lesbian content). Here's a list of ten publishers who produce predominantly female- and lesbian-content books:

> *Alyson Books*
> *Aunt Lute Books*
> *Bella Books*
> *Cleis Press*
> *New Victoria Publishers*
> *Odd Girls Press*
> *Seal Press*
> *Women's Work Press, LLC*
> *The Naiad Press*
> *WW Norton*

— GAY ICON AT A GLANCE: —
JUDY GARLAND

BORN: Frances Ethel Gumm on 10 June 1922 in Grand Rapids, Michigan, USA
DIED: 22 June 1969 in London, England
MARRIAGES: David Rose (1941–45)
    Vincente Minnelli (1945–51)
    Sidney Luft (1952–65)
    Mark Herron (1965–66)
    Mickey Deans (1969)

CHILDREN: Liza Minnelli (born 12 March 1946)
    Lorna Luft (born 21 November 1952)
    Joey Luft (born 29 March 1955)

CAREER HIGHLIGHTS...
'Dear Mr Gable' • Dorothy in *The Wizard Of Oz* • 'Over The Rainbow' • 'Let's Put On A Show!' • 'The Trolley Song' • *Easter Parade* • 'Get Happy' • The London Palladium • 'Hello, everyone. This is Mrs Norman Maine' • 'The Man That Got Away' • Capitol Records • *The Judy Garland Special* • Las Vegas • Dominion Theatre • *Judgment At Nuremburg* • Carnegie Hall • *The Judy Garland Show* • Five Grammys at Carnegie Hall • 'The Battle Hymn Of The Republic' • June 1969 • Stonewall • Frank Campbell's Funeral Chapel

— MONKEY BUSINESS —

It's now a well-known fact that chimpanzees are our closest kin when it comes to a DNA map. However, it's less well known that there are some chimps who display other attributes close to our hearts. Lesbianism is extensively practised by the pygmy chimpanzee, often known as the bonobo.

— THE STONEWALL RIOTS: — GAY RIGHTS MAKE NEW YORK HEADLINES

'Village Raid Stirs Melee'
– New York Post, 28 June 1969

'4 Policemen Hurt in "Village" Raid; Outbreak By 400 Follows A Near-Riot Over Raid'
– New York Times, 29 June 1969

'Police Again Rout "Village" Youths'
– New York Times, 30 June 1969

'Gay Power Comes To Sheridan Square'
– Village Voice, 3 July 1969

'Homo Nest Raided, Queen Bees Are Stinging Mad'
– New York Daily News, 6 July 1969

'The Gay Anger Behind The Riots'
– New York Post, 8 July 1969

— PULP FICTION PART 1 —

In 1950, the first pulp-fiction lesbian-themed books from the publisher Fawcett Crest appeared, kicking off with Tereska Torres's *Women's Barracks*. The books invariably ended unhappily and contained all the angst and torment you would expect from that genre of popular fiction, but they were nevertheless important instruments for lesbians around the USA in that they served as affirmations that their readers were not alone.

— I'LL TAKE PAUL LYNDE TO BLOCK —

Between 1968 and 1979, funny man Paul Lynde held court in the centre square of *Hollywood Squares*, a popular daytime game show. Lynde was a veteran Broadway performer who at the time was best known for his role as the harried father in the stage and film version of *Bye Bye, Birdie*. He later became a familiar face on sitcoms (most memorably as Samantha's Uncle Arthur on *Bewitched*) and TV variety shows such as *Donny And Marie*. He was at his best, however, when he was sitting in the centre of a giant tic-tac-toe board tossing out one-liners and zingers, which earned him two Emmys in 1975 and 1979 for Outstanding Individual Achievement in Daytime Programming.

Lynde was perhaps the gayest man on American television in those days, although it wasn't something people back then ever acknowledged. Of course, he didn't have to; just take a look at a small sample of his responses to questions he was asked by *Squares* host Peter Marshall:

PM: 'When Richard Nixon was Vice-President, he went someplace on a "goodwill mission", but instead wound up being stoned and shouted at. Where did this take place?'
PL: 'Pat's room.'

PM: 'Paul why do Hell's Angels wear leather?'
PL: 'Because chiffon wrinkles too easily.'

PM: 'During the War of 1812, Captain Oliver Perry made the famous statement "We have met the enemy and..." What?'
PL: 'They are cute.'

PM: 'In *The Wizard Of Oz*, the lion wanted courage and the tin man wanted a heart. What did the scarecrow want?'
PL: 'He wanted the tin man to notice him.'

PM: 'What do you call a man who gives you diamonds and pearls?'
PL: 'I'd call him darling.'

PM: 'Paul, in what famous book will you read about a talking ass who wonders why it's being beaten?'
PL: '*The Joy Of Sex*.'

PM: 'Paul, can anything bring tears to a chimp's eyes?'
PL: 'Finding out Tarzan swings both ways.'

PM: 'Paul, Snow White – was she a blonde or a brunette?'
PL: 'Only Walt Disney knows for sure.'

PM: 'Paul, at what age does a person understand the true meaning of a spanking?'
PL: 'The true meaning? Twenty-three.'

PM: 'According to legend, who looks better, a pixie or a fairy?'
PL: 'Well, looks aren't everything.'

PM: 'According to the French chef Julia Child, how much is a pinch?'
PL: 'Just enough to turn her on...'

PM: 'According to the old song, what's breaking up that old gang of mine?'
PL: 'Anita Bryant.'

— 'SWF WLTM SWF, GSOH ESS': THE EARLY DAYS —

In the early 1900s, the Dutch weekly newspaper *Pst-Pst* began to carry lineage adverts which are today recognised as some of the earliest documented examples of lesbian personal ads.

— ADAM AND YVES: DON'T LET THIS HAPPEN! —

Inspired by the success of the 1978 gay French comedy *La Cage Aux Folles* in the United States, writer/producer Danny Arnold (*Barney Miller*) pitched his idea for a sitcom about a gay couple to ABC. When the network announced in 1979 that they were developing Arnold's show, tentatively titled *Adam & Yves*, conservative Christian groups sprang into action and started a letter-writing campaign demanding that the network should refuse to pick up the series. They even distributed pre-printed postcards to send to ABC that featured on the front a photograph of two children watching TV above the slogan 'ABC Presents Perverted Filth: Don't Let This Happen!'. On the flip side, the postcard, addressed to ABC President Elton Rule, stated, 'I hereby request that you refuse to carry ABC's proposed homosexual comedy series, *Adam And Yves*, or any similar program.'

Arnold and the network lost interest in the project in 1980, but that didn't stop the campaign. By 1982, ABC reportedly received a total of 100,000 postcards protesting against a television series that never existed.

— ONLINE LESBIAN SEARCH TOOLS —

Here's a list of websites that should help you to search all of dykedom online:

www.femina.com
www.feminist.com
www.gay.com
www.lesbianindex.com
www.lesbianation.com
www.lesbian.org
www.planetout.com/search/
www.wowwomen.com
www.womyn.org

— COMING OUT (AND DOWN) —

Coming Out, the first (and only) gay-themed film produced in East Germany, is the story of a schoolteacher in East Berlin who begins to question his sexuality when he is reunited with an old school chum with whom he once had an affair. Unlike most coming-out stories, this one doesn't have the typical 'isn't it great to be gay' ending.

The film was well received when it premiered on 9 November 1989. During the premiere party, the film's director, Heiner Carow, heard shouting and cheering outside the theatre. At first he assumed that the party had spilled out into the streets, but he soon learned that the crowd was celebrating another momentous occasion: the tearing down of the Berlin Wall.

— CHINESE LIBERATION —

In April 1992, two lesbians who had been living together in China were charged with 'unruly behaviour' on the basis of their cohabitation and were imprisoned for two weeks. In an unprecedented act of official liberal attitudes, the Ministry of Public Security ordered their release and later announced that there is no legal basis for forbidding lesbians from cohabiting.

By November, the Chinese government stated that same-sex acts would no longer be regarded as an offence against 'social order'.

— TV PARENTS COME OUT —

Since the 1990s, gay and lesbian television characters in dramatic series and sitcoms are no longer reduced to the role of the sassy gal pal or co-worker. We've started to see more of a variety of regular and recurring gay and lesbian characters, some of whom are also mums and dads.

- DAVID (Dan Castellanta) and WILLIAM (Sam McMurray), Francine's (Tracey Ullman's) gay dads in *The Tracey Ullman Show*.

- JUSTIN (Christopher Malcolm), Saffron's (Julia Sawalha's) dad in *Absolutely Fabulous*.

- MICKEY TUPPER (Paul Dooley), Martin's (Brian Benben's) dad in *Dream On*.

- SUSAN BUNCH (Jessica Hecht) and CAROL WILLIG (Anita Barone/Jane Sibbet), mothers to Ross's (David Schwimmer's) son Ben in *Friends*.

- BEV HARRIS (Estelle Parsons), Roseanne Connor's (Roseanne Barr's) mother in *Roseanne*.

- LAURIE MANNING (Lisa Darr), Holly's mother in *Ellen*;

- SAMANTHA SANDERS (Christine Belford), Steve's (Ian Ziering's) mother in *Beverly Hills, 90210*.

- Butch Gamble (John Goodman), Charlie's (Greg Pitts's) father in *Normal, Ohio*.

- ROMEY SULLIVAN (Esther Hall) and LISA LEVENE (Saira Todd), Alfred's mothers in *Queer As Folk* (UK).

- MELANIE MARCUS (Michelle Clunie) and LINDSAY PETERSON (Thea Gill), Gus's mothers in *Queer As Folk* (US).

- SIMON BANKS (Christopher Sieber) and PHILLIP STODDARD (John Benjamin Hickey), Liz's gay dads in *It's All Relative*.

- JUDITH HARPER (Marin Hinkle), Jake's (Angus T Jones's) mother in *Two And A Half Men*.

— 'TIL DEATH DO THEM PART —

In January 1892, US newspapers reported widely on 17-year-old Freda Ward's murder by her lover, 19-year-old Alice Mitchell. Both Freda and Alice were upper-class Memphis society girls who had entered into a pact never to separate. Their relationship was unacceptable to their families, with Ward's family refusing Alice contact with Freda. Alice subsequently met with Freda on a train and slashed her throat, ensuring that the pact was kept. Alice Mitchell was later found insane and was committed to an asylum.

This was one of the first times that lesbianism was discussed in the US media on a widespread basis, and it became the ideal vehicle with which to cite the dangers of same-sex love. This ghoulish story, and its unhappy ending, was to be echoed in many books and films over the ensuing decades.

— *THE BOYS IN THE BAND* —

This groundbreaking play by Mart Crowley ushered in a new era for the representation of gay men in both theatre and the cinema. In his *New York Times* review, critic Clive Barnes described the play as 'by far the frankest treatment of homosexuality I have ever seen on the stage... This is not a play about a homosexual, but a play that takes the homosexual milieu, and the homosexual way of life, totally for granted, and uses this as a valid basis for the human experience. Thus it is a homosexual play, not a play about homosexuality, by taking an honest and, at times, painful look at modern gay life.'

The Boys In The Band premiered off-Broadway at Theater Four on Sunday 14 April 1968. The play was produced by Richard Barr and Charles Woodward, and directed by Robert Moore. The play's original cast also appeared in the film, which was adapted for the screen by Crowley and directed by William Friedkin, and was released in the United States on 17 March 1970.

THE CAST
Michael ....Kenneth Nelson
Alan ....Peter White
Harold...Leonard Frey
Emory ....Cliff Gorman
Donald...Frederick Combs

Hank ....Laurence Luckinbill
Larry ....Keith Prentice
Cowboy ....Robert La Tourneaux
Bernard..Reuben Greene

FIRST MODERN USE OF THE WORD 'LESBIAN'
— IN ENGLISH —

Written by William King and published in Ireland in 1732, 'The Toast' was a searing piece of satirical poetry addressing a group of Dublin socialites. At one point it makes use of the term 'lesbian loves', constituting one of the earliest uses of the word *lesbian* in English to connote same-sex sexual relationships.

— THE FILM ROLES OF —
MISS BARBRA JOAN STREISAND

ROLE	MOVIE	YEAR
Fanny Brice	*Funny Girl*	1968
Mrs Dolly Levi	*Hello, Dolly*	1969
Daisy Gamble	*On A Clear Day You Can See Forever*	1970
Doris	*The Owl And The Pussycat*	1970
Judy Maxwell	*What's Up Doc?*	1972
Margaret Reynolds	*Up The Sandbox*	1972
Katie Morosky Gardner	*The Way We Were*	1973
Henrietta Robbins	*For Pete's Sake*	1974
Fanny Brice	*Funny Lady*	1975
Esther Hoffman	*A Star Is Born*	1976
Hillary Kramer	*The Main Event*	1979
Cheryl Gibbons	*All Night Long*	1981
Yentl/Anshel	*Yentl*	1983
Claudia Draper	*Nuts*	1987
Dr. Susan Lowenstein	*The Prince Of Tides*	1991
Rose Morgan	*The Mirror Has Two Faces*	1996
Mrs Focker	*Meet The Fockers*	2004

— FIRST UK LESBIAN MAGAZINE —

In 1964, women from the Minorities Research Group founded *Arena Three*, considered to be the UK's first lesbian magazine.

— DIVAS THANK THEIR GAY FANS —

'They can easily connect with intensity and emotion – whether it is about love or enjoying life or anything that comes from the gut. I think they can feel that my music comes from that place. It comes from my gut.'

— *Britney Spears, 2004*

'My gay audience has been with me from the beginning. The most important thing to me is that it was a very natural coming together. In recent years a lot of record companies market directly towards "the pink pound", but I never did that. They kind of adopted me instead.'

— *Kylie Minogue, 2004*

'My gay fans have been so loyal and so great. Gay fans usually love you when you're in the dumps, in the toilet – they're still there for you. I have a very Judy Garland feeling.'

— *Cher, 1999*

'I love the gay fans. They're the best fans. I've been around gay people since I entered this business. They are the most energetic, loyal and appreciative audience. As a performer, you are very lucky to have a following like that.'

— *Celine Dion, 1998*

'I have a lot of gay following, and still do, and I love them as much as they love me.'

— *Donna Summer, 1995*

'My gay audience is as important to me as my pumps... I don't feel whole unless I have on five-inch pumps. I don't feel whole unless I have a gay crowd.'

— *Patti LaBelle, 1994*

'When I got into trouble with the government, it was the transvestites and the gay world who kept my name alive because they were imitating me all the time. And there is nothing in the world more flattering than being flattered by imitation.'

— *Eartha Kitt, 2000*

— COLONY FELONY —

In the early days of the settlement of the USA by Europeans, it seems that lesbian practices were not unknown...

- On 5 December 1642, a servant from Massachusetts was sentenced to be whipped for 'unseemly practices' with another woman. This is the first documented instance of legal prosecution in colonial North America for lesbian-sex relations.

- On 6 March 1649 in Plymouth, Massachusetts, two married women were charged with 'lewd behaviour, each with other upon a bed'. Charges were dropped against one but the other, Sara Norman, was required to publicly confess her 'unchaste behaviour'.

- Massachusetts was not the only state in which this occurred. By 1656, the New Haven law code made Connecticut the first of the American colonies to make same-sex acts between women punishable by death.

— LANDMARK DECISIONS —

13 JANUARY 1958 – *ONE, INC, VS OLESEN, POSTMASTER OF LOS ANGELES*, 355 US 371

In 1953, ONE, Inc, one of the early post-war gay rights groups, started publishing *ONE* magazine, a widely circulated publication for its day, featuring articles, fiction, reviews and 'Letters To The Editor'. The magazine played an integral role in achieving one of the organisation's main goals: to bring homosexuals around the country closer together.

The US Postal Office decided that *ONE* magazine was obscene and therefore could not be distributed through the mail. The plaintiffs cited the following portions of the October 1954 issue as evidence:

- A story entitled 'Sappho Remembering' which is 'lustfully stimulating' to the homosexual readers;

- A poem entitled 'Lord Samuel And Lord Montagu' which contains 'filthy language';

- An ad for a Swiss publication *The Circle* that gives information 'for the obtaining of obscene matter'.

— LANDMARK DECISIONS (CONT'D) —

Over the next few years, the case made its way through the courts. In 1958, the US Supreme Court overturned a ruling of the US Court of Appeals for the Ninth Circuit (*Roth vs United States*, 354 US 476), thus lifting the ban.

---

22 MAY 1967 – *BOUTILIER VS IMMIGRATION AND NATURALIZATION SERVICE*, 387 US 118
12 APRIL 1983 – *HILL VS IMMIGRATION AND NATURALIZATION SERVICE*

In 1966, a Canadian named Clive Michael Boutilier was deported by the Immigration and Naturalization Service because he was homosexual and, therefore, 'afflicted with psychopathic personality' and 'excludable from admission into the United States' under Section 212(a)(4) of the Immigration and Nationality Act of 1952. Boutilier had been living in the United States for eight years when he petitioned for naturalisation. During the proceedings, he admitted to having been arrested (but never convicted) of sodomy in 1959. During the INS's investigation, Boutilier admitted that he had had homosexual experiences prior to entering the United States.

Boutilier's petition to the Court of Appeals for the Second Circuit was denied by a 3–1 vote. In stating the majority opinion, Judge Kaufman held that the decision was not a judgment on the plaintiff's character but an interpretation of the 1952 statute. Judge Moore dissented, stating that the interpretation of the law used by the INS is 'not only offensive to but, in my opinion, completely lacking in due process', because their conclusion that Boutilier was 'afflicted with psychopathic personality' was made without an examination by a psychiatrist.

The decision was upheld by the US Supreme Court by a 6–3 vote. In his opinion for the court, Justice Clark wrote that the term 'psychopathic personality' was not vague and was included in the law to exclude homosexuals from entry into the United States. In his dissenting opinion, Justice Douglas stated that the term 'psychopathic personality' is a treacherous one like 'communist' or, in an earlier day, 'Bolshevik'.

The 1952 law was overturned in 1983 in a case involving a British journalist, Carl Hill, who, upon entering the country, stated that he was a homosexual to an INS officer. Hill was brought in front of an immigration judge, who ruled against deportation because there was no medical evidence that Hill was 'afflicted with a sexual deviation or mental defect'. The Ninth District Court of Appeals upheld the ruling, stating that in their opinion Congress did intend the INS to obtain a Public Medical Health Certificate before deporting homosexuals on the ground of affliction with a psychopathic personality, sexual deviation or mental defect.

---

30 JUNE 1986 – *BOWERS VS HARDWICK*, 478 US 186
26 JUNE 2003 – *LAWRENCE VS TEXAS*, 539 US 558

In 1982, the Atlanta police were let into the home of Michael Hardwick by a house guest. When the police entered Hardwick's bedroom, he was performing oral sex on another man. The police arrested Hardwick for sodomy under a Georgia sodomy law that carries up to a 20-year sentence for anyone who 'performs or submits to any sexual act involving the sex organs of one person and the mouth or anus of another'. The district attorney chose not to press charges, but Hardwick felt that the law violated his constitutional rights and took his case to the District Court, where it was dismissed. Hardwick appealed to the United States Court of Appeals, which reversed the ruling. The case was argued in front of the Supreme Court, which upheld Georgia's state sodomy law as constitutional in a 5–4 decision. In concurring with the Court's opinion, Chief Justice Burger stated that sodomy laws have 'ancient roots' and that 'in constitutional terms there is no such thing as fundamental right to commit homosexual sodomy'.

Seven years later, the Supreme Court, in a 6–3 decision, declared Texas's sodomy laws as unconstitutional. As in the Hardwick case, the police, responding to a reported weapons disturbance, entered the home of John Lawrence, where they observed him engaging in anal intercourse with another man, Tyron Garner. Both men were charged and convicted under a Texas statute that makes it a crime for two persons of the same sex to engage in certain intimate sexual conduct. Their convictions were upheld in criminal court and the Court of Appeals, and were then reversed by the Supreme Court. The majority opinion stated that the Texas statute violated Lawrence and Garner's vital interests in liberty and privacy. In his majority opinion, Justice Kennedy wrote, 'The liberty protected by the Constitution allows homosexual persons the right to choose to enter upon relationships in the confines of their homes and their own private lives and still retain their dignity as free persons.'

At the time that the decision was handed down, 13 states still had sodomy laws on their books. Both heterosexual and homosexual sodomy was illegal in nine states, while the remaining four had sodomy statutes only for homosexual sex. Following the Supreme Court ruling on the *Lawrence vs Texas* case, all existing sodomy laws in the United States are unconstitutional.

— MADONNA'S US DISCOGRAPHY —

ALBUM	RELEASE DATE	PEAK POSITION (ALBUM)	SINGLE	PEAK POSITION (SINGLE)
Madonna	July 1983	8	'Holiday'	16
			'Borderline'	10
			'Lucky Star'	4
Like A Virgin	Nov 1984	1	'Like A Virgin'	1
			'Material Girl'	2
			'Angel'	5
			'Dress You Up'	5
Vision Quest (soundtrack)			'Crazy For You'	1
True Blue	June 1986	1	'Live To Tell'	1
			'Papa Don't Preach'	1
			'True Blue'	3
			'Open Your Heart'	1
			'La Isla Bonita'	4
Who's That Girl (soundtrack)	July 1987	7	'Who's That Girl'	1
			'Causing A Commotion'	2
You Can Dance	Nov 1987	14		
Like A Prayer	March 1989	1	'Like A Prayer'	1
			'Express Yourself'	2
			'Cherish'	2
			'Oh Father'	20
			'Keep It Together'	8
I'm Breathless	May 1990	2	'Vogue'	1
			'Hanky Panky'	10
Immaculate Collection	Nov 1990	2	'Justify My Love'	1
			'Rescue Me'	9
Erotica	Oct 1992	2	'Erotica'	3
			'Deeper And Deeper'	7
			'Bad Girl'	36
			'Rain'	14
Bedtime Stories	October 1994	3	'Secret'	3
			'Take A Bow'	1
			'Bedtime Story'	4
			'Human Nature'	46

Album	Release date	Peak position (album)	Single	Peak position (single)
Something To Remember	Nov 1995	6	'You'll See'	6
			'Love Don't Live Here Anymore'	78
			'This Used To Be My Playground'	1
			'I'll Remember'	2
Evita (soundtrack)	Nov 1996	2	'You Must Love Me'	18
			'Don't Cry For Me, Argentina'	8
Ray Of Light	March 1998	2	'Frozen'	2
			'Ray Of Light'	5
			'Power Of Goodbye'	11
			'Nothing Really Matters'	93
Music	Sept 2000	1	'Music'	1
			'Don't Tell Me'	4
GHV2	Nov 2001	7	'Beautiful Stranger'	19
American Life	April 2003	1	'American Life'	37
			'Die Another Day'	8

Source: *Billboard* magazine

— FEMALE SEED —

The cannabis plant is predisposed to become either male or female, although in the quest for high concentrations of the psychoactive THC (delta-9-tetrahydrocannabinol, the active ingredient in marijuana) the female plants are most coveted. Experimentation by cannabis breeders has led to genetic modification in order to achieve the most potent chromosomally XX (ie female) plant, which is forced by the hormone gibberellic acid to produce male flowers, whose pollen contains only X chromosomes. When this pollen is offered to another female plant, there is a 100% certainty that it will produce only female seed.

— THE GAY JESUS MOVIE —

In April 2000, a phony email petition started circulating in protest of an upcoming film that depicted Jesus and his disciples as homosexuals. The author stated that some European countries had already banned the film and encouraged recipients to 'send this to ALL of your friends to sign to stop the movie from coming out'. Of course, the petition is not addressed to any person or company. The original email message does mention the play *Corpus Christi* by Terrence McNally, which was targeted by protestors when it ran in New York City in August of 1998. There have been no plans to turn the play into a film.

— THE LABRYS —

Used as both a weapon and a harvesting tool in ancient European, African and Asian matriarchal societies, the labrys is a double-sided hatchet or axe and a symbol of strength and self-sufficiency in the lesbian and feminist community. Greek artwork depicts labrys weapons borne by the Amazon armies of Europe, who were known to be ferocious and merciless in battle but, once victorious, ruled with justice. Amazon rule was based on a dual-queen system, whereby one queen was in charge of the army and battle and the other queen stayed behind to administer the conquered cities. In Greek mythology, Demeter (the goddess of the Earth) used a labrys as her sceptre, and rites associated with her worship and that of Hecate (the goddess of the Underworld) are believed to have involved lesbian sex. These days, many a dyke's neck will be adorned with a labrys necklace.

— URNING —

In 1862, German gay activist Karl Heinrich Ulrichs devised the term *Urning* (*Uranian*), based on a passage in Plato's *Symposium*, where 'Uranian' referred to a member of what the Greek called a 'third sex' – a person with 'a feminine soul confined in a masculine body' or vice versa. The term and the very concept gained a popular following and usage in Europe and North America over the next few decades. The concept of a third sex was explored in books such as John Radclyffe Hall's *The Well Of Loneliness*, in which the author suggests that homosexuality is more a result of birth than of choice, due to its proponents being members of an intermediate third sex.

— AB FAB —

This British sitcom created by Dawn French and Jennifer Saunders has achieved a strong cult following among gay men, who no doubt relate to Edina Monsoon (Saunders) and her gal pal, Patsy (Joanna Lumley), and their antics. In today's age of safe sex and political correctness, Edina and Patsy take us back to a time when it was OK to booze it up, get stoned and have a bit of fun. Edina's long-suffering, neglected daughter, Saffron (Julia Sawalha) – better known to her mother as 'Sweetie Darling' – is the only voice of reason. Compared to her free-spirited mother, she is somewhat shy and sexually repressed.

- *Ab Fab* was based on a sketch that appeared on the TV show *French And Saunders*, in which Dawn French plays a teenager trying to do her homework but keeps getting interrupted by her drama-queen mother (Saunders).

- The first episode, 'Fashion', debuted on BBC2 on 12 November 1992. The series jumped over to BBC1 where it continued for five more seasons for a total of 31 episodes and several specials. There may soon be a sixth season.

- A French (as in France) film version of *Absolutely Fabulous*, entitled *Absolument Fabuleux*, was released in 2001. The cast featured Josiane Balasko (Eddie Mousson), Nathalie Baye (Patricia), Marie Gillain (Safrane) and Claude Gensac (Mamie Mousson). Saunders and Catherine Deneuve make cameo appearances.

— KAMA SUTRA —

Written in India around AD400, *The Kama Sutra*
describes harem lesbianism and thereby popularised
the idea that it was rife in most harem societies.
The degree to which such practices existed is
uncertain, although the mention of it indicates that
it was at least considered possible.

— PROFESSIONAL GAY AND LESBIAN ASSOCIATIONS —

Association of Gay and Lesbian Psychiatrists (US)

Gay and Lesbian Association of Doctors and Dentists (UK)

Gays and Lesbians in Foreign Affairs Agencies (US)

Gay and Lesbian Medical Association (US)

Gay, Lesbian, and Straight Education Network (US)

International Association of Lesbian and Gay Judges

International Association of Lesbian/Gay Pride Coordinators

National Lesbian and Gay Journalists Association(US)

National Lesbian and Gay Law Association (US)

*National Organization of Gay and Lesbian Scientists and Technical
Professionals (US)*

Society of Lesbian and Gay Anthropologists (US)

— CHINA DOLLS —

Like those of the rest of the world, in Chinese historical documents male
homosexuality is far more common than lesbianism. However, there are a
few accounts which evidence a long history of lesbian sexuality in China:

- Documents dating from AD193, including *Records Of The Han*, allude
  to the existence of sexual relationships between women living in the
  Han emperor's palace.

- Sex manuals written during the Ming dynasty (1368–1644) go into some
  detail about how lesbian acts could be incorporated with heterosexual

intercourse for men with multiple concubines. Lesbian sex is frequently portrayed in erotic prints of the day and artificial aids for vaginal and clitoral stimulation also existed at this time.

• The Golden Orchid Associations were formed on the back of the silk industry and had an exclusively female membership in which a lesbian couple could choose to engage in a marriage ceremony whereby one partner became the 'husband' and the other the 'wife'. There was an associated party with gifts and a feast, and which was attended by their female friends as witnesses to the event. The couple were free to adopt young girls, who could then inherit family property from the couple's parents. This was apparently a reasonably common practice in the 19th-century Guangzhou province, the only other alternative to not marrying a man being the Buddhist nunnery.

This movement lasted until the Japanese invasion of 1937 and at their peak the Golden Orchid Associations had more than 100,000 members. They were largely funded by the women's ability to support themselves by working in the lucrative silk-spinning industry, thereby demonstrating the dependencies between a woman's economic situation and her marital choice.

— TRIBADE OR NOT TRIBADE —

By around 1600, the word *tribade* (from the Greek *tribein*, meaning 'to rub') began to be used in western Europe to describe women who engaged in sexual relations with other women. Initially, this referred only to obtaining sexual pleasure through friction against bodies, but it later came to mean (and to be used more generally as meaning) lesbian.

— HOMOSEXUALITY AND THE BLACKLIST —

In the late 1940s through the 1950s, hundreds of men and women suspected or known to be communists or communist sympathisers were put on the Hollywood Blacklist, which prevented them from getting work in the film industry. Included on the list were the names of bisexual and gay men, although the reason why they were blacklisted was not so much their sexual orientation as their leftist leanings.

— HOMOSEXUALITY AND THE BLACKLIST (CONT'D)—

On 5 May 1953, director/choreographer Jerome Robbins appeared in front of the House Un-American Activities Committee (HUAC) as a friendly witness. Robbins was gay and allegedly agreed to testify for fear of the truth coming out. He admitted to being a member of the Communist Political Association from 1944 to 1947 because it was fighting fascism and, therefore, anti-Semitism. Among the names Robbins gave to the committee were those of writer/producer Edward Chodorov; theatre/film character actor Lloyd Gough, who invoked the Fifth Amendment when he was called to testify; and actor Madeline Lee, the wife of actor Jack Gilford, who was also blacklisted.

Meanwhile, composer Leonard Bernstein (1918–1990), who is best known for his scores for *On The Town* and *West Side Story*, was one of the 151 names that appeared in *Red Channels*, a pamphlet that listed the names of writers, directors and actors who had been members of leftist organisations but had not yet been officially blacklisted. The list also included composers Marc Blitzstein, who admitted in a closed session that he was a member of the Communist Party but refused to name names; and Aaron Copland, who testified that he was never a communist.

Actor Will Geer, who would become known to television audiences in the 1970s as the grandfather on *The Waltons*, refused to answer any questions after being named. He told the Committee that he was declining to answer any questions because of 'the situation of the world as it is. It's a hysterical situation.'

— PIONEERING LESBIAN WRITERS —

Gertrude Stein
Hilda Doolittle (HD)
Willa Cather
Virginia Woolf
Vita Sackville-West
Radclyffe Hall
Colette
Emily Dickinson
Selma Lagerlöf
Renée Vivien

— SEX LIKE AN EGYPTIAN —

In around 2200BC, an Egyptian book about women's dreams included references to two women having sex with one another.

Two thousand four hundred years later, in AD200, a spell recorded on papyrus fragments is documented, designed to make a woman called Sarapias fall in love with another woman, Herais. It is one of several such spells recorded.

— 'TO KEEP MYSELF PHYSICALLY STRONG, — MENTALLY AWAKE, AND MORALLY STRAIGHT'

In June 2000, the US Supreme Court ruled by a 5–4 vote that the Boy Scouts of America can bar homosexuals (as well as atheists and agnostics) from being scout leaders because forcing the movement to accept them violates its constitutional right of freedom of association and free speech under the First Amendment. In his decision on behalf of the majority, Chief Justice William H Rehnquist stated that 'homosexual conduct is inconsistent with the values it seeks to instil' and that, while homosexuality has gained greater acceptance, 'the first Amendment protects expression, be it of the popular variety or not'.

The decision stems from a long legal battle between the Scouts and James Dale, who was barred in 1990 from being an adult leader because he was gay and, therefore, not morally straight. In light of the Supreme Court's decision and the Scouts' refusal to change its discrimination policy against gays and atheists, many municipalities and charity organisations – including chapters of the United Way – around the country withdrew their financial support from their local scout troops.

APHRA BEHN, EARLY NOVELIST AND — DEFENDER OF LESBIANISM —

In 1688, Aphra Behn – considered by many to be the first professional woman writer – wrote the poem 'To the Fair Clarinda, Who Made Love to Me, Imagined More than Woman', in which she defended her sexual attraction to a young woman.

— TWO MUMS MAKE BABIES —

In April 2004, Japanese scientists from Tokyo University of Agriculture reported the birth of Kaguya, a baby mouse created by using two genetic mothers – a first in the world of mammals. The scientists used a procedure that, for technical and ethical reasons, cannot be replicated in people, so it's not likely to erase the need for the male in human reproduction. One of the mothers was a mutant newborn whose DNA had been altered to make it behave like a male contribution to an embryo. The significance in this research is not the potential that two mums can make babies but that stem cells can be harvested and used in the treatment of a variety of diseases.

— CANADIAN GAY AND LESBIAN ARCHIVES —

- **Canadian Gay and Lesbian Archives (www.clga.ca)** – Toronto archive founded in 1993 containing 5,300 files of information on Canadian and non-Canadian events, individuals and organisations.

- **Hall–Carpenter Archives (http://hallcarpenter.tripod.com/)** – Named after author Marguerite Radclyffe Hall and Edward Carpenter, the Hall–Carpenter Archives comprises the main collection in the Archives Division of the London School of Economics Library, the Lesbian and Gay Newsmedia Archive at Middlesex University and the National Sound Archive at the British Library.

- **Homodok (www.homodok.nl)** – The largest gay, lesbian, bisexual, transgender and queer library collection in the Netherlands, with branches in Amsterdam and Leeuwarden.

- **Human Sexuality Collection (rmc.library.cornell.edu/HSC/)** – Collection housed in Cornell University Library in Ithaca, New York, containing materials related to gay life, human sexuality and the American gay-rights movement since Stonewall.

- **International Gay Information Center Archives (www.nypl.org/research/chss/spe/rbk/igic.html)** – This archive in the New York Public Library consists of 40 collections pertaining to the history and culture of gay men and lesbians, and to the history of the AIDS/HIV epidemic.

- **June L Mazer Lesbian Archives (www.lesbian.org/mazer/)** – Located in West Hollywood, California, the Mazer Archives contains books, periodicals and video and audio tapes, as well as the entire photography files of Dana Press.

- **ONE National Gay and Lesbian Archives (www.oneinstitute.org)** – The world's largest research library on gay, lesbian, bisexual and transgender heritage and concerns.

— LESBIAN AND BISEXUAL PAINTERS —

Tamara de Lempicka
Rosa (Marie Rosalie) Bonheur
Hannah Gluckstein ('Gluck')

— FIVE REASONS WHY GAY MEN LOVE — DAME ELIZABETH ROSEMOND HILTON WILDING TODD FISHER BURTON BURTON WARNER FORTENSKY TAYLOR

1 Taylor is a survivor who keeps on going, despite losing second husband Michael Todd in a plane crash, double pneumonia, rehab at the Betty Ford Clinic, a hip replacement, a benign brain tumour, numerous back injuries and countless operations.

2 Taylor is a tireless AIDS activist who founded The Elizabeth Taylor AIDS Foundation, which has distributed over $8 million to AIDS organisations around the world.

3 Taylor is a brilliant actor. Just watch *Who's Afraid Of Virginia Woolf?* and *Cat On A Hot Tin Roof*.

4 Taylor doesn't take herself too seriously. After winning two Academy Awards, she created the role of Helena Cassadine in *General Hospital*; played Wilma's mother, Pearl Slaghoople, in the film version of *The Flintstones*; and played herself in several sitcoms, including *Here's Lucy*, *The Nanny*, *The Simpsons*, *Murphy Brown* and *High Society*.

5 Taylor has been gay-friendly from the beginning. She was a loyal friend to Montgomery Clift, Roddy McDowell and Rock Hudson.

— THE TEDDY WINNERS —

The Teddy Award is given each year at the Berlin International Film Festival
to a gay- and/or lesbian-themed feature film. Here's a list of its past recipients:

2004 *Wild Side* (dir Sébastien Lifshitz)

2003 *Mil Nubes de Paz Cercan El Cielo, Amor, Jamás Acabarás de Ser
      Amor* (1,000 *Peace Clouds Encircle The Sky, Love, You Will Never
      Stop Being Love*) (dir Julián Hernández)

2002 *Walking On Water* (dir Tony Ayres)

2001 *Hedwig And The Angry Inch* (dir John Cameron Mitchell)

2000 *Gouttes D'eau Sur Pierre Brûlantes* (*Water Drops On Burning
      Rocks*) (dir François Ozon)

1999 *Fucking Åmål* (dir Lukas Moody)

1998 *Yue Kuai Le, Yue Duo Lo* (*Hold You Tight*) (dir Stanley Kwan)

1997 *All Over Me* (dir Alex Sichel)

1996 *The Watermelon Woman* (dir Cheryl Dunye)

1995 *The Last Supper* (dir Cynthia Roberts)

1994 *Go Fish!* (dir Rose Troche)

1993 *Wittgenstein* (dir Derek Jarman)

1992 *Together Alone* (dir PJ Castellaneta)

1991 *Poison* (dir Todd Haynes)

1990 *Coming Out* (dir Heiner Carow)

1989 *Looking for Langston* (dir Isaac Julien)
      Fun Down There (dir Roger Stigliano)

1988 *The Last Of England* (dir Derek Jarman)

1987 *The Law Of Desire* (dir Pedro Almodóvar)

— SORORITY SISTERS —

Lambda Delta Lambda was the first lesbian sorority at an American
University, founded in 1988 at the University of California at Los Angeles
(UCLA). Its members aimed to highlight awareness of women's, gay and
minority issues.

— YOU ARE INVITED TO THE WEDDING OF... —

In 1971, a bogus invitation to the wedding of actor Rock Hudson to Jim Nabors, US TV's Gomer Pyle, made its way around Hollywood and into the hands of the tabloids and gossip columnists, who had a field day 'outing' the couple. The joke didn't hurt Hudson's career, but Nabors' variety show was cancelled at the end of the 1971 season. He eventually moved to Hawaii, where he owns a 500-acre macadamia nut plantation.

As for the hoax, apparently 500 of the invitations were sent by a gay couple in Huntington Beach to their annual party. Each year, they would send out joke invitations stating something like, 'You are invited to the coronation of Queen Elizabeth in Huntington Beach.'

— FRENCH LETTERS —

French literature of the mid to late 19th century was some of the earliest modern literature to accept and promote lesbianism, albeit as being somewhat exotic and decadent. In 1867, poet Charles Baudelaire published his now famous *Les Fleurs du Mal*, which included poems exoticising lesbians, one of whom is Sappho. This was followed in 1894 by Pierre Louÿs's *Les Chansons de Bilitis* (*The Songs Of Bilitis*), where Bilitis is a fictitious character living on Lesbos during the time of Sappho and who recites lesbian love poetry.

— SCREWING IN LIGHTBULBS —

Q: How many lesbians does it take to screw in a light bulb?
A: That's not funny...

Q: How many lesbians does it take to screw in a light bulb?
A: Light? Who needs light? We prefer to do it in the dark!

Q: How many lesbians does it take to screw in a light bulb?
A: Five. One to screw it in and four to bitch about the man who invented it.

Q: How many lesbians does it take to change a light bulb?
A: Fifty. One to actually do it and 49 to write a folk song about it.

Q: How many S/M dykes does it take to change a light bulb?
A: Two. A bottom to do the job and a top to tell her what to do.

— SOME BILLIE JEAN KING FIRSTS —

• First woman *Sports Illustrated* 'Sportsperson of the Year', 1972.

• First female athlete to win over $100,000 prize money in a single season.

• First outspoken athlete for women and their right to earn comparable money in tennis and other sports.

• Established the first successful women's professional tennis tour.

• Only woman to win US singles titles on all four surfaces: grass, clay, indoor and hard.

— INDIGO GIRLS ALBUM DISCOGRAPHY —

All That We Let In (2004)
Become You (2002)
Retrospective (2000)
Come On Now Social (1999)
Shaming of The Sun (1997)
1,200 Curfews (1995)
Swamp Ophelia (1994)
Rites Of Passage (1992)
Back On The Bus, Y'All (1991)
Nomads Indians Saints (1990)
Strange Fire (1989)
Indigo Girls (1989)

— GLAAD MEDIA AWARD WINNERS —

The Gay and Lesbian Alliance Against Defamation (GLAAD) is a non-profit organisation dedicated to promoting and ensuring fair, accurate and inclusive representation of gay and lesbian people and events in the media, as a means of eliminating homophobia and discrimination based on gender identity and sexual orientation. Since 1990, GLAAD has been honouring individuals and projects in the media and entertainment industries for their balanced and accurate representations of the lesbian/gay/bisexual/transgender communities and

the issues that affect their lives. Here's a list of those shows
that have been recognised by GLAAD:

Year	Feature film(s)	TV drama	TV comedy
1990		Heartbeat	Doctor, Doctor
1991	The Handmaid's Tale	LA Law	Doctor, Doctor
	Longtime Companion	LA Law	Doctor, Doctor
1992	Frankie And Johnny		Roseanne
	Fried Green Tomatoes At The Whistle Stop Café		
1993		Melrose Place	Roseanne
1994	Philadelphia	Sisters	Dream On
	Hsi yen		
1995	The Adventures Of Priscilla, Queen Of The Desert	My So-Called Life	Friends
	Go Fish!		Roseanne
1996	Boys On The Side	NYPD Blue	
	The Incredibly True Story Of Two Girls In Love		
1997	Bound	Chicago Hope	Spin City
	Beautiful Thing		
1998	In And Out	NYPD Blue	Ellen
	My Life In Pink		
1999	Gods And Monsters	Chicago Hope	Will And Grace
	High Art		
2000	Being John Malkovich	Dawson's Creek	Will And Grace
	Boys Don't Cry		
2001	Billy Elliot	Queer As Folk	Will And Grace
	Broken Hearts Club		
2002	The Mexican	Six Feet Under	Will And Grace
	Hedwig And The Angry Inch		
2003	The Hours	Six Feet Under	Will And Grace
	Kissing Jessica Stein		
2004	Bend It Like Beckham	Playmakers	Sex And The City
	Yossi And Jagger		

— A QUESTION OF LOVE —

The title of the 1978 made-for-TV drama about a lesbian's battle to win custody of her son. Directed by Jerry Thorpe and starring Gena Rowlands and Jane Alexander, *A Question Of Love* was based on the story of Mary Jo Risher, who was found unfit to be a mother because she was a lesbian. The movie was nominated for a Golden Globe in 1978, in the category Outstanding Production Television Movie. Mary Jo Risher's tale was the subject of Gifford Guy Gibson's 1977 book *By Her Own Admission: A Lesbian Mother's Fight To Keep Her Son* (Garden City, Doubleday).

— BORN BUTCH —

The opening words of American Actress Charlotte Cushman's (1816–76) memoirs are 'I was born a tomboy'. Butch from the beginning, she was said to crack open the heads of her dolls to examine their brains. She was linked in romantic friendship to a series of artistic women: American painter Rosalie Scully, English poet Eliza Cook and American sculptor Emma Stebbins (with whom her relationship lasted 20 years).

— GAY PORN FILM TITLES —

A Beautiful Behind (2002)
Accounts Layable (2001)
All About Steve (1994)
All Male Ass Attack (1998)
All the Right Boys (1985)
The Bare Dick Project (2000)
The Best Little Whorehouse in TEX-ASS (2001)
Blow Your Own Horn (1989)
Boys With A Hood (1994)
Brazilian Butt Camp (2003)
Cumming Clean (2002)
Cummin' Of Age (1994)
Czech In And Out (1997)
Czech Is In The Male (1998)
Everybody Does Raymond (2000)
The Florida Erection (2001)
How The West Was Hung (1999)

Jacuzie Park (1994)
Mantasy Island (1998)
Monsters And Size Queens (1999)
My Best Friend's Woody (1998)
Nine-Inch Males (2001)
The Object Of My Erection (1998)
Queer Eye For The GI (2004)
Riding Boys In Cars (2003)

— BOYS BEWARE! —

A 1961 educational film entitled *Boys Beware* was shown in some American schools to warn boys about homosexual child molesters.

The first scenario involves a boy named Jimmy, who is befriended by a man named Ralph. The narrator tells us that Ralph is 'sick…a sickness that was not visible like smallpox, but no less dangerous and contagious'. Ralph takes Jimmy fishing and buys him gifts. As Ralph leads Jimmy into a motel room, the narrator explains that 'payments were expected in return. Jimmy didn't recognise that.'

'All homosexuals are not passive,' the narrator warns, 'some resort to violence.' This is the case in the second scenario, in which young Mike accepts a ride from a friendly, nicely dressed stranger. 'He probably never realised until too late that he was riding in the shadow of death.'

The other scenarios depict boys being followed out of public restrooms ('a hangout for homosexuals') and getting tricked into getting into a man's car. 'One never knows when the homosexual is about,' the narrator concludes. 'He may appear normal and it may be too late when you discover he is mentally ill.'

Boys Beware is part of the Prelinger Archives, a collection of short advertising, educational, industrial and amateur films. You can watch it online (for free) at www.archive.org.

— HOLLYWOOD LESBIANS —

The 1966 premiere of the movie *The Group* saw the first use of the word *lesbian* in a Hollywood feature.

— THE FERRO-GRUMLEY AWARDS —

The Ferro-Grumley Awards recognise excellence and experimentation in literary fiction. They were first awarded in 1990 and are made possible by the estates of novelists and lovers Robert Ferro (*The Family Of Max Desir*) and Michael Grumley (*Life Studies*). Each award is given for books published in the preceding year in the USA or Canada. Past female winners are:

YEAR	AUTHOR	BOOK
2004	Nina Revoyr	*Southland*
2003	Carol Anshaw	*Lucky In The Corner*
2002	Emma Donoghue	*Slammerkin*
2001	Sarah Waters	*Affinity*
2000	Judy Doenges	*What She Left Me*
1999	Patricia Powell	*The Pagoda*
1998	Elana Dykewoman	*Beyond The Pale*
1997	Persimmon Blackbridge	*Sunnybrook*
1996	Sarah Schulman	*Rat Bohemia*
1995	Heather Lewis	*House Rules*
1994	Jeanette Winterson	*Written On The Body*
1993	Dorothy Allison	*Bastard Out Of Carolina*
1992	Blanche McCrary Boyd	*The Revolution Of Little Girls*
1991	Cherry Muhanji	*Her*

— BIGGUS DICKUS —

As avid readers of 1950s beat literature, Donald Fagen and Walter Becker decided to name their band Steely Dan after a giant dildo in William Burrough's novel *Naked Lunch*. With their first album under this name titled *Can't Buy A Thrill*, the band comprised Donald Fagen (keyboards and vocals), Walter Becker (bass), Jeff 'Skunk' Baxter (guitar), Jim Hodder (drums) and David Palmer (vocals).

— HIGHWAY ROBBERY —

Moll Cutpurse was a notorious master-thief highway robber active in 17th-century London. Various conjecture exists about her homosexuality, with references made to her female 'companions'. Born Mary Frith in 1584, she was sent to work as a servant after refusing to go to school. She rebelled, began to dress as a man, carry a sword and turn to petty crime. Described as a bully, pickpocket, fortune-teller, receiver and forger, she somehow managed to avoid being brought before the courts. Eventually she became the head of a gang of thieves and was later convicted of robbing and wounding a general. She was sent to Newgate Prison in punishment, from which payment of £2,000 damages secured her release. Following this brush with the law, she ran a pawnshop in Fleet Street where people could recover their own stolen goods.

Moll Cutpurse became a figure of popular myth, dying in 1659 when she was 75 years old. Three years later, her purported autobiography was published, although there is much debate as to it being her original work. There are three sections to this text: one addressed 'To The Reader', a longer introductory section and a 'Diary'.

The figure of Mary Frith appeared in plays such as Middleton and Dekker's *The Roaring Girl* and Nathan Field's *Amends For Ladies*.

THE ULTIMATE DIVA DISCO DANCE PARTY
— MIX TAPE —

SONG	ARTIST	DURATION
'I Love The Night Life (Disco 'Round)'	Alicia Bridges	5:34
'Don't Leave Me This Way'	Thelma Houston	5:40
'Finally'	Ce Ce Peniston	4:01
'If I Can't Have You'	Yvonne Elliman	2:59
'Do You Wanna Funk?'	Sylvester	6:49
'No More Tears (Enough is Enough)'	Donna Summer & Barbra Streisand	4:43
'Lady Marmalade'	Patti LaBelle	3:56
'The Boss'	Diana Ross	3:48
'I Am What I Am'	Gloria Gaynor	3:12
'Get Dancin''	Disco Tex & The Sexolettes	3:53
'Love Hangover'	Diana Ross	3:47
'MacArthur Park'	Donna Summer	3:55
'Disco Inferno'	The Trammps	3:35
'It's Raining Men'	The Weather Girls	5:26
'We Are Family'	Sister Sledge	3:35
'More, More, More'	Andrea True Connection	3:09
'Shake Your Grove Thing'	Peaches & Herb	5:32
'I Will Survive'	Gloria Gaynor	8:00
'Last Dance'	Donna Summer	3:18

TOTAL RUNNING TIME: 85:26

— THE SHOW MUST GO ON —

Emily Sailers and Amy Ray make up the out and politically active folk rock duo The Indigo Girls.

August 14 2003 is remembered as the day that Manhattan and much of northeastern United States and Canada lost all of their electrical power, which understandably threw the entire region into panic and crisis, with most scheduled concerts cancelled when acts were unwilling or unable to perform without electricity.

Not so for The Indigo Girls. Not prepared to see their legion of faithful fans disappointed, the show went on. A small generator, and the request that their fans cram closer to the stage, was all that Amy Ray and Emily Sailers needed to perform at the Central Park Summerstage gig in New York City. Only sundown put an end to the show, for reasons of public security and safety.

— LENGTH OF THE FEMALE ORGASM —

While few women have timed the duration of a climax to sexual excitation, according to scientific reports the female orgasm lasts, on average, between six and ten seconds. There have been a few extreme cases that report 'more than 20 seconds', which begs the question, with gradual increases in human performance, will women in the near future be carried along on waves of bliss for more than half a minute? And will they need to train for the privilege?

— WHAT DO YOU CALL A YOUNG LESBIAN? —

Baby butch (mid-late '60s)
Boy dyke
Baby dyke (late '60s)
Camper (late '60s)
Dinky dyke
Gay chick (1971)
Semi-diesel

— DRAG QUEEN HALL OF FAME —

CANDY DARLING (JAMES LAWRENCE SLATTERY) (1946–74)

Warhol superstarlet who as a child started imitating the female Hollywood movie stars she watched on *The Million Dollar Movie*. On moving to Manhattan, she started getting hormone shots and became a full-time drag queen. She appeared in two of Warhol Factory director Paul Morrissey's films: *Flesh* (1970) and *Women In Revolt* (1971). She is also the 'Candy who came out from the island' in Lou Reed's 'Walk On The Wild Side'. She died of cancer in 1974 at the age of 28.

DIVINE (GLEN MILSTEAD) (1945–88)

Baltimore transvestite who teamed up with her high-school pal John Waters in a series of comedies that redefined the meaning of the word 'camp'. Her early films with director Waters were made on a shoestring budget and pushed the envelope when it came to taste. Some of her more memorable roles include teenager Dawn Davenport in *Female Trouble* (1974), suffering housewife Francine Fishpaw in *Polyester* (1981) and loving mother Edna Turnblad in *Hairspray* (1988).

CHARLES LUDLAM (1943–87)

Actor, playwright, and founder of the Ridiculous Theater Company in Greenwich Village. His troupe performed camp versions of classical texts like *Hamlet* and *Finnegans Wake* as well as stage variations of *Camille* and *Sunset Boulevard* (retitled *Screen Test*), in which Ludlam imitated Norma Desmond.

CHARLES PIERCE (1926–99)

Entertainer known for his impersonations of Hollywood legends such as Gloria Swanson, Bette Davis, Tallulah Bankhead and Joan Crawford. In addition to his nightclub act, in the late 1970s and '80s the 'Master and Mistress of Surprise or Disguise' did an occasional TV guest spot (*Starsky And Hutch*, *Laverne And Shirley*) and film roles (including female impersonator Bertha Venation in Harvey Fierstein's *Torch Song Trilogy*). Pierce died of cancer in 1999 at the age of 72.

CRAIG RUSSELL (1948–90)

Toronto-born performer known for his impersonations of Bette Davis, Judy Garland, Carol Channing and Mae West (he was West's secretary/companion in the late 1960s). Russell won Best Actor at the Berlin Film Festival for his role as a female impersonator in Robin Turner's *Outrageous!* He died due to AIDS in 1990.

— LAMBDA —

The lambda symbol was chosen in the early days of the gay and lesbian emancipation movement as a gay symbol, and there has been a vivid debate that persists until today as to why. Here's a short history about what is known – and a little about what's been speculated.

- The symbol was first chosen as a gay motif in 1970, when it was adopted by the New York Gay Activists Alliance and subsequently, in 1974, by the International Gay Rights Congress, held in Edinburgh. These two adoptions led to a widespread acceptance of the lambda symbol as being representative of the gay and lesbian political movement.

- Lambda is the Greek lower-case letter L, which some say stands for *liberation*.

- Others have held that in physics lambda represents energy, which correlates to the energy of the gay and lesbian political movements.

- Yet others believe that lambda denotes wavelength, and that members of the gay and lesbian communities are on a different one.

- Lambda has also been used to represent scales and balances.

- The ancient Greek Spartans regarded lambda to mean unity, while the Romans considered it 'the light of knowledge shed into the darkness of ignorance'.

Despite arguments over its origin and its reason for being a universally accepted symbol for gays and lesbians, the usage of the lambda symbol as such is undisputed.

— SOME LESBIAN MAILING LISTS —

www.christianlesbians.com/emaillist.html
www.userhome.com/etheridge (for the irrepressible Melissa fan)
www.gimpgirl.com/lists/index.html (for dykes with disabilities)
www.lesbianation.com
www.lesbian.org/lesbian-lists
www.apocalypse.org/pub/sappho

— DIFFERENT FROM THE OTHERS —

In the 1919 German silent film *Anders als die Anderen* (*Different From The Others*), a concert violinist is blackmailed by a man he once took home with him from a party. When the violinist reports the crime to the police, he is also sent to prison for violating Germany's anti-sodomy law, Paragraph 175. When he gets out of jail, the violinist discovers that his career has been ruined by the scandal and commits suicide. In the final scene, Dr Magnus Hirschfeld, who was leading the campaign to repeal Paragraph 175, delivers an impassioned speech in which he asks the audience to 'take heed' because 'the time will come when such tragedies are no more. For knowledge will conquer prejudice, truth will conquer lies and love will triumph over hatred!'

This early example of pro-gay propaganda was considered a lost film; there were no known prints to be in existence. However, in the late 1970s, a copy of the film was discovered in Russia by German film critic and journalist Manfred Salzberger. The surviving print was actually a shortened version of the original that was released in 1927 as part of a longer film entitled *Gesetze der Liebe* (*The Laws Of Love*). The abbreviated version of *Anders als die Anderen* was shown at gay film festivals around the country and on public television in the 1980s.

— THE PINKY RING —

The fashion of wearing a ring (usually gold) on the little finger of the left hand has long been a way of answering the queer-or-not question. It grew in popularity during the '50s, '60s and early '70s, and some believe it has ancient roots and mythical qualities because the little finger represents spirituality.

— A DAY WITH(OUT) ART —

On 1 December 1989, Visual AIDS, the New York-based collective of artists that launched the Red Ribbon Project, sponsored the first 'Day Without Art'. On this day of national mourning, art galleries and museums around the USA closed their doors while staff members went out in the community working as volunteers at local AIDS organisations. In 1997, Visual AIDS recommended that 1 December be changed to a 'Day With Art', and museums and galleries now stay open on that date to display the work of artists who live with HIV/AIDS, as well as AIDS-themed art projects.

— 'OUT' TENNIS GIRLS —

These tennis professionals from the past and present have been outed from the players'-room closet. Their outing has not always been of their own volition and has happened either during or after their playing career. Some have gone on to acknowledge the declaration publicly and others have let us speculate forever.

Martina Navratilova (USA)*
Billie Jean King (USA)
Amelie Mauresmo (France)*
Conchita Martinez (Spain)*
Beatriz 'Gigi' Fernandez (Puerto Rico)
Yana Novotna (Czech Republic)
Hana Mandlikova (Aus)
Helen Hull Jacobs (USA)

* Denotes players that continue to play on the WTA circuit.

— THE RAINBOW FLAG —

Today this widespread, well-known symbol of gays and lesbians flies above most gay establishments as a beacon to the weary (and thirsty) traveller. Its origins as a gay symbol, however, are relatively recent.

The Rainbow Flag as we know it today was developed by San Francisco artist Gilbert Baker in 1978 to meet the need for a gay symbol which could be used (and re-used later) for the San Francisco Gay and Lesbian Pride Parade. Baker's primary inspiration was the Rainbow Coalition flag of the black civil-rights movement, on whose design the now universally adopted eight-stripe banner was based. Baker used different colours to represent different aspects of gay and lesbian life:

- Hot pink for sexuality;
- Red for life;
- Orange for healing;
- Yellow for the sun;
- Green for nature;
- Blue for art;
- Indigo for harmony;
- Violet for spirit.

The story goes that Baker and 30 volunteers hand-stitched and hand-dyed prototype flags for the 1978 parade. However, when Baker took his design to the San Francisco Flag Co to have it mass-produced for the 1979 parade, the hot-pink stripe had to go: he'd hand-dyed the colour and pink was not commercially available.

— GENDER SYMBOLS —

Gender symbols representing men and women have existed for a considerable period. Symbols like those shown were given to each of the Roman gods. Each consists of a circle with a symbolic identifier attached. The circle with an arrow attached at roughly the two-o'clock position stands for Mars, the god of war, and is a strong symbol of masculinity, thus the symbol has come to represent men. The circle with the cross extending downwards is a symbol of femininity representing Venus (Aphrodite), the goddess of love and beauty, and as you'd expect has come to represent women. Join two women symbols together, or two of the men symbols together, and you get two lovely icons to represent women who love women and men who love men. From about the early 1970s onwards, the usage of these symbols became widespread.

— GAY ICON AT A GLANCE: —
BARBRA STREISAND

BORN: Barbra Joan Streisand, 24 April 1942, Brooklyn, New York
MARRIAGES: Elliot Gould (1963–71)
James Brolin (1998–)
CHILDREN: Jason Gould (born 1966)

CAREER HIGHLIGHTS...
Miss Marmelstein • *The Barbra Streisand Album* • *The Third Album* • *The Judy Garland Show* • Fanny Brice • *A Christmas Album* • *A Happening in Central Park* • 'Happy Days Are Here Again' • 'Hello, Gorgeous' • Dolly Levi • *Stoney End* • *The Way We Were* • 'Evergreen' • Duets with Neil Diamond, Donna Summer and Barry Gibb • *Yentl* • *The Broadway Album* • *The Prince Of Tides* • 'Like Buttah' • The Concert • The Clintons • www.barbra-streisand.com • AFI Lifetime Achievement Award

— PRESUMABLY STRAIGHT DIRECTORS WITH GAY — SENSIBILITIES

BOB FOSSE (1927–87)

Dancer turned choreographer turned film director who directed only five films yet managed to reinvent the movie musical not once but twice: first by integrating the songs and story in the screen version of *Cabaret* (1972), which made Liza Minnelli a star (and won them each an Oscar); and then by turning his own life story into the self-reflexive, modernist musical *All That Jazz* (1979).

JOSEPH LOSEY (1909–84)

American-born director who studied theatre under Bertolt Brecht and later moved to England after being blacklisted in 1951 for not appearing in front of the House Un-American Activities Committee (he was in Italy directing *Stranger On The Prowl* at the time). His films often focus on characters who, like himself, are outsiders (his best film, 1963's *The Servant*, deals with a man's masochistic relationship with his manservant), while at the same time he also has a camp side, both intentionally (*Modesty Blaise* [1966]) and not (*Boom!* [1968]).

DOUGLAS SIRK (1897–1987)

German director who started his career in the 1930s at UFA but fled Germany when Hitler rose to power. In the 1950s, he directed a series of melodramas for Universal Studios that exposed the hypocrisy of post-war bourgeois society. Sirk's trademark is his excessiveness, particularly in terms of music and colour, which he uses to express the emotions of his conflicted characters. His list of top moneymakers includes *Imitation Of Life* (1959), *Magnificent Obsession* (1954), *Written On The Wind* (1956) and *All That Heaven Allows* (1955).

JOSEPH L MANKIEWICZ (1909–83)

Mankiewicz directed *A Letter To Three Wives* (1949), *All About Eve* (1950), *Suddenly Last Summer* (1959) and *Cleopatra* (1963). Enough said.

KEN RUSSELL (BORN 1927)

British-born director who was in the Royal Air Force, danced with the Ny Norsk Ballet and trained as a photographer before pursuing a career as a producer and director. Russell became known for his lavish, excessive directorial style and his willingness to push the envelope in dealing with provocative subject matter and themes. Among his best films are *Women In Love* (1969), which features the famous nude wrestling scene between Alan Bates and Oliver Reed; *The Music Lovers* (1970), a film bio of gay composer Tchaikovsky; *Tommy* (1975), the film version of The Who's rock opera; and the provocative and entertaining *Crimes Of Passion* (1984).

WILLIAM WYLER (1902–81)

One of the most celebrated directors in American film history, Wyler's range of credits includes westerns (*The Westerner* [1940]), literary and dramatic adaptations (*Wuthering Heights* [1939], *These Three* [1936] and his remake of *The Children's Hour* [1961]), melodramas (*The Best Years of Our Lives* [1946]) and musicals (*Funny Girl* [1968]). Although he is not considered a 'women's director' in the same vein as George Cukor, many of his films focus on strong female characters played by actresses such as Bette Davis, Greer Garson, Audrey Hepburn and Barbra Streisand, who usually took home a statue at Oscar time.

WOLFGANG PETERSEN (BORN 1941)

Can you name one female actor who has appeared in a Wolfgang Petersen film? Of course not, because Petersen's best films focus on his male characters and their bodies in motion, whether they be at sea (ie German U-boat commander Jurgen Prochnow and his sweaty crew in *Das Boot* [1981], Captain George Clooney and sexy first mate Mark Wahlberg in *The Perfect Storm* [2000]) or at war (Brad Pitt and his beefy castmates in *Troy*) – not to mention one of the director's early films, a screen adaptation of Alexander Ziegler's controversial novel *The Consequence*, which focuses on a gay convict's love affair with a prison warden's son.

— PULP FICTION PART 2 —

In 1957, Ann Bannon published the paperback original *Odd Girl Out*, the first of four pulp novels that depicted lesbian life during the era lived by the characters Beth, Laura and – from the second book in the series onwards – Beebo.

Today, *Odd Girl Out*, *Women In The Shadows* and *Beebo Brinker* are considered classics of early contemporary lesbian fiction. They give a sense of what it must have been like for a young butch lesbian to leave Hicksville for New York's Greenwich Village and served as a manual for young lesbians, who later flocked to cities around the USA in pursuit of just such a lifestyle. The popularity of the books was in part due to satisfying straight-male fantasies, but also in letting isolated lesbians around the USA know that there were other women out there just like them.

While dated by today's standards, Bannon's books were early pioneers of reality-based lesbian writings and paved the way for the likes of Rita Mae Brown and Isabel Miller.

— WOMEN'S LIB BEGINS —

On 19 July 1848, Elizabeth Cady Stanton and co-
organiser Lucretia Mott invited several hundred
women to Seneca Falls, New York, for the first
Women's Rights Convention. About 100 people
signed a 'Declaration of Sentiments' – modelled on
the Declaration of Independence – representing the
beginning of organised feminism in the US.
However, it wasn't until nearly half a century later
that women were given the franchise and
substantially longer still before lesbians had any
rights at all.

— SO YOU WANT TO IMPRESS A SOFTBALL CHICK? —

Softball has long been one of those sports that lesbians know that lesbians
play. As such, the bleachers surrounding any pitch are often filled by adoring
female fans. While adoring the chicks that play the game, the self-same
appreciation of the rules might not always exist. For any softball chicks who
need to know more about the game itself, here are a few tips on what 'getting
to first base' really means:

- Softball is played around bases by batting and running in the hope you'll
  score.

- Points are scored by runs, which are awarded when someone on the
  batting team touches all bases, including home, without being out.

- The team that scores the highest number of runs in the allotted number
  of innings wins.

- The pitcher uses an underhand throwing motion.

- When the fielding team makes three outs, the teams switch over such
  that the fielding team then bats and the batting team plays the field.

- An 'out' is made by the batter striking out, a fielder catching a fly ball
  or the runner being tagged or forced out at a base.

It might help to know that the game originated in 1887 when a bunch of
blokes in Chicago hit a tied-up boxing glove around with a broomstick.

— YAOI AND SLASH FICTION —

Animé is a Japanese-developed style of animation known for its futuristic settings, violence and sex. One of the most popular forms of *animé* and comics (*manga*) is the *yaoi*, which focuses on male–male relationships between boys or young men in a romantic and sexually explicit manner. Written by female writers, *yaoi* is popular among girls because the stories are romantic and the boy characters are usually *bishounen*, a Japanese word that literally means 'beautiful boy' and refers to a specific Japanese concept of beauty (slender and effeminate or androgynous in appearance).

Yaoi, pronounced 'yah-oh-ee' (all vowels are pronounced), is an acronym for *Yama nashi, Imi nashi, Ochi nashi'*, meaning 'no climax, no meaning, no resolution'. In English, the acronym phrase is translated as 'Plot? What Plot?', meaning that the minimal plot is there only as an excuse for the characters to have sex.

In the male–male relationships depicted in *yaoi*, one partner is dominant while the other is submissive:

• The *seme* is the dominant partner in the relationship;
• The *uke* is the submissive partner in the relationship.

The symbols 'X' and '+' refer to the type of story:

• X indicates that the story is sexually explicit;
• + means that the story is romantic.

The symbols appear between the two names, with the name of the dominant partner coming first, followed by that of the submissive partner, ie:

• Michael X Gabriel means the story is sexually explicit;
• Michael + Gabriel means the story is romantic.

Sometimes *yaoi* take male characters who are already established and pair them together in a sexual or romantic relationship. This is nothing new; in America, it's more commonly known as *slash fiction*, a form of fan fiction that involves the gay pairing of two characters outside their original text – eg *Star Trek*'s Kirk and Spock as a homosexual couple.

Finally, in *yaoi* an intimate, highly sexual relationship is designated as 'lemon', while a 'no-lemon' relationship is more platonic.

— DAVID'S NAUGHTY BITS —

To mark the 3,000th anniversary of David's conquest of Jerusalem, the city of Florence presented Jerusalem with a replica of Michelangelo's famous statute of David. Religious leaders considered the nude statue to be pornographic, so Florence commissioned a second, fully clothed replica to be sent in its place.

— DYKES TO WATCH OUT FOR —

This is the title of a long-running comic strip born in 1983 from the imagination and observation of author Alison Bechdel. *Dykes To Watch Out For* pictorially describes the life and times of Mo and her friends, who set out to explore and illuminate late-20th-/early-21st-century issues from every angle imaginable. Foreign policy, domestic routine, parenting practice, love, sex and just about everything else is graphically questioned and manages to strike a chord with every lesbian who reads it. Ten book-length *Dykes To Watch Out For* collections have been compiled, as follows:

Dykes To Watch Out For (1986, Firebrand Books)
More Dykes To Watch Out For (1988, Firebrand Books)

New, Improved Dykes To Watch Out For (1990, Firebrand Books) 1991*

Dykes To Watch Out For: The Sequel (1992, Firebrand Books) 1992*

Spawn Of Dykes To Watch Out For (1993, Firebrand Books) 1993*

Unnatural Dykes To Watch Out For (1995, Firebrand Books)

Hot Throbbing Dykes To Watch Out For (1997, Firebrand Books)

Split-Level Dykes To Watch Out For (1998, Firebrand Books)

Post-Dykes To Watch Out For (2000, Firebrand Books)

Dykes And Sundry Other Carbon-Based Life-Forms To Watch Out For (2003, Alyson Publications) 2003*

* *Denotes that collection being awarded the Lambda Literary Award for Lesbian and Gay Humour for that particular year.*

— THE VILLAGE PEOPLE —

This popular '70s disco act was the brainchild of producers Henri Belolo and Jacques Morali, who according to legend got the idea for the group at a costume party at a Greenwich Village disco. They pulled together six singers, put them in assorted costumes (the group's trademark) and composed songs for them that were full of gay double entendres.

- **The Indian** – Felipe Rose.

- **The GI** – Alex Briley.

- **The Cowboy** – Randy Jones, who married his lover of 20 years, recording artist Will Grega.

- **The Construction Worker** – David Hodo.

- **The Leatherman** – Glenn Hughes, who died in 2001 of lung cancer and was buried in his outfit.

- **The Policeman** – Victor Willis, who quit and was replaced by Ray Simpson, brother of Valerie Simpson of Ashford & Simpson.

— LESBIAN SCI-FI, FANTASY AND HORROR WRITERS —

In recent years, sci-fi, fantasy and horror writing has become increasingly popular in the field of lesbian fiction in a way that only mystery and romance can match. Many argue that its rise is due to the sexual ambivalence allowed in words of the imagination, or that the genre permits a redefinition of societal norms. Both points are probably true, and there are other arguments equally valid. Contemporary lesbian authors who have recently excelled within this genre include:

Katherine V Forrest
Laura Adams (Karin Kallmaker)
Melissa Scott
Nicola Griffith
Jewelle Gomez
Gael Baudino
Antoinette Azolakov

— LESBIAN ARCHITECTS —

Architecture, like many professional areas, has long been the domain of men, and to a large degree it still is. Nevertheless, women have made significant inroads upon this profession, and some of these women have possibly been lesbians. Here are some early noteworthy female architects who were probably (but not conclusively) lesbian:

ELSIE DE WOLFE (1865–1950)
De Wolfe is considered by many as the first professional interior designer. She brought light colours and casual décor into formerly dark, heavy, Victorianesque interiors.

JULIA MORGAN (1872–1957)
Morgan was the first woman architect registered in California. Her best-known work is 'San Simeon', or Hearst Castle, which is a mix of European and American elements.

ELEANOR RAYMOND (1887–1989)
Raymond was considered an innovator and was interested in solar power and new structural technologies. Her primary work is found in small modern homes in New England, USA.

— SUMMER OLYMPIC WOMEN'S TEAM SPORTS —
INAUGURATION YEAR WINNERS

Sport	Women's Inauguration Year	Men's Inauguration Year	Gold Medallist	Silver Medallist	Bronze Medallist
Basketball	1976	1936	Soviet Union	USA	Bulgaria
Field hockey	1980	1908	Zimbabwe	Czecho-slovakia	Soviet Union
Soccer	1996	1900	USA	China	Norway
Water polo	2000	1900	Australia	USA	Russia

— HEATHER'S MOMMIES AND DADDY'S ROOMMATE —

In 1990, Alyson Publications, a gay press, launched a new imprint of books written specifically for children of gay and lesbian parents. The first two books released were *Heather Has Two Mommies*, by Lesléa Newman, and *Daddy's Roommate*, written and illustrated by Michael Willhoite. Both books were soon making newspaper headlines as parents and educators campaigned to get the books removed from school and community libraries because they were anti-family (because they dealt with divorce) and condoned homosexuality. Consequently, the two books hit the Number 1 and Number 2 slots on the American Library Association's list of banned books. In 1994, Senators Jesse Helms (R-NC) and Robert Smith (R-NH) sponsored a measure that would deny federal funding to schools that 'implement or carry out a programme that has either the effect of encouraging or supporting homosexuality as a positive lifestyle alternative'. On the Senate floor, Smith said that the books were 'graphic' and 'obscene'.

— BOBBIE SOX —

Janis Joplin's 'Me And Bobbie McGee' was rumoured to be about a woman.

— WHAT'S FUNNY ABOUT LESBIANS? —

Despite a legacy of not being particularly light-hearted, there are a number of lesbian artists who have bucked this trend in an attempt to see the funnier side of life. Here are some of these pioneers:

ARTIST	PRIMARY MEDIUM
Erika Lopez	Writer (books)
Ellen Galford	Writer (books)
Alison Bechdel	Cartoonist (books)
Ellen Orleans	Writer (books)
Lily Tomlin	Actor/stand-up performer
Rhona Cameron	Actor/stand-up performer
Rosie O'Donnell	Talk-show host/comedienne
Sandra Bernhardt	Stand-up performer
Ellen DeGeneres	Sitcom actress and stand-up performer
Amanda Bearse	Sitcom actress
Kate Clinton	Stand-up performer
Marga Gomez	Stand-up performer
Suzanne Westenhoefer	Stand-up performer
Karen Williams	Stand-up performer

— WHAT GOES ON UNDER THE COVERS —
STORY 'BLURBS' FROM THE COVERS OF GAY-THEMED PAPERBACK NOVELS OF THE 1950s AND 1960s

'The story of men who are different'
Strange Brother (1952) by Blair Niles

'He had to choose – a half world or a world of woman's love'
Man Divided (1954) by Dean Douglas

'Part story, part heartbeat, part lowdown song, about the guys who pay the price for everything...'
Lonely Boy Blues (1956) by Alan Kapelner

'A surging novel of forbidden love'
The Tormented (1956) by Audrey Erskine Lindop

'They lived in fear, loved in secret.'
Twilight Men (1957) by André Tellier

'Was their relationship too intimate? What would you decide?'
Never The Same Again (1958) by Gerald Tesch

'Most men fall in love with women, but some men fall in love with themselves!'
Muscle Boy (1958) by Bud Clifton

'Twilight lives of talent and torment, made-man-for-man in the world of dance'
Mr Ballerina (1961) by Ronn Marvin

'Women lusted after this handsome virile jazzman... It took him years of agony to realise he wanted a man.'

'This time his partner is a man.'
Hot Pants Homo (1964) by Percy Fenster

'A lover and his lady...and his laddie'
AC/DC Stud (1965) by Victor Jay

'He burned with a lust passion as he soared into the ecstasy of love – but this time his partner was a man.'
So Sweet, So Soft, So Queer (1965) by Victor Jay

'He came to camp!'
Stranger At The Door (1967) by Don Holliday

— FINE-ART PAINTINGS OF LESBIANS —

Gabrielle d'Estrée And	Second School of Fontainebleau, *circa* 1594
The Duchesse de Villars	
Jupiter And Callisto	Peter Paul Rubens, 1613
Two Nymphs In A Landscape	Palma il Vecchio, 1516–1518
Sleep	Gustave Courbet, 1866
Sirens	Charles Edouard Boutibonne, 1883
In Summertime	Eliseu Visconti, 1891
Sleep	Georges Callot, 1895
Sleep	Ida Teichmann, 1905
Fond Confessions	Louis de Schryver, 1905
Nest Of Sirens	Adolphe La-Lyre, *circa* 1906
After The Bath	Pierre-Georges Jeanniot, 1908
The Echo	Jean-François Auburtin, 1911
The Two Friends/Tenderness	Egon Schiele, 1913
Just A Couple Of Girls	Harry Wilson Watrous, 1915

— THE BLACK TRIANGLE —

The pink triangle – a symbol rooted in the Nazi persecution of gay men during World War II – has come to represent gay and, often, lesbian lifestyles. Perhaps less well known, however, is the black triangle, which has a similar heritage. Unlike gay men, lesbians were not included in the German Paragraph 175 prohibition of homosexuality, but they were nevertheless ordered by the Nazis to wear a black triangle designating prisoners exhibiting 'anti-social behaviour'. The very ideal of Nazi womanhood was centred upon children, kitchen and the Church, so the acts of lesbianism and prostitution constituted, in Nazi eyes, this kind of behaviour. It is held that many lesbians wore the black triangle as a result of this determination, and since the 1970s it has come to be representative of lesbians and feminists.

— BILLIE JEAN KING: A BRIEF BIOGRAPHY —

• Born Billie Jean Moffitt, 22 November 1943, Long Beach, California.

• In her early years she was an exceptional softball player, but she moved on to professional tennis, becoming a household name.

• In 1965 she married Mr Lawrence King and since then has been better known under her husband's family name.

• In 1967 Billie Jean was named Outstanding Female Athlete of the World.

- She is credited with being one of the first female athletes to speak out against sexual inequality in organised sports. On September 20 1973, in what was billed as 'The Battle of the Sexes', she defeated 55-year-old Bobby Riggs 6–4, 6–4, 6–3 before 30,492 spectators in the Houston Astrodome.

- She is one of only eight players to hold a singles title in each of the Grand Slam tennis events.

- In 1971, King (still married) began an affair with Marilyn Barnett, a hairdresser. When she became the subject of a 'galimony' lawsuit ten years later, King acknowledged the affair and thereby became the first American athlete to acknowledge openly a homosexual relationship. She later divorced.

- In 2001, King received an award from GLAAD (Gay and Lesbian Alliance Against Defamation) – an organisation devoted to reducing discrimination against homo- and bisexuals – for 'furthering the visibility and inclusion of the community in her work'. The award noted her involvement in production and the free distribution of educational films, as well as serving on the boards of several AIDS charities.

- In 1987, she was inducted into the International Tennis Hall of Fame in Newport, Rhode Island.

- In 1990, *Life* magazine named her one of the '100 Most Important Americans of the 20th Century'.

- In 1998, King finally came out officially as a lesbian in an interview with the US gay and lesbian magazine *The Advocate*. While she had acknowledged her homosexual affair in 1991, until the publication of this article she hadn't outwardly proclaimed an ongoing acceptance of herself as an out lesbian.

- In March 2000, GLAAD awarded King the Capitol Award for her service to the LGBT community.

BILLY JEAN KING – MAJOR GRAND SLAM TOURNAMENTS WON
Australian Open...One singles title
French Open...One singles title
Wimbledon championships........Six singles titles (20 titles overall)
US Open...Four singles titles

— SPORTS AT THE FIRST GAY GAMES, 1982 —

Basketball
Billiards
Bowling
Boxing
Cycling
Diving
Golf
Marathon
Physique
Powerlifting
Soccer
Softball
Swimming
Tennis
Track and field
Volleyball
Wrestling

— HOMOPHOBIA HALL OF SHAME: ANITA BRYANT —

Bryant is a singer and former beauty queen (second runner-up in the 1959 Miss America pageant) who had two hits back in the late 1950s and 1960s: 'Paper Roses' in 1958 and 'My Little Corner Of The World' in 1960. She became a familiar face on US TV as the spokeswoman for the Florida Citrus Commission ('Come to the Florida Sunshine Tree') and on commercials for Coca-Cola, Kraft Foods, Holiday Inn and Tupperware.

In 1977, Dade County, Florida, passed a human-rights ordinance granting homosexuals equal protection under the law. Bryant spearheaded a campaign to get a referendum on the ballot to repeal the law by making one false and reprehensible statement after another:

- *On homosexuals:* 'As a mother, I know that homosexuals cannot biologically reproduce children; therefore, they must recruit our children.'

- *On gay rights:* 'If gays are granted rights, next we'll have to give rights to prostitutes and to people who sleep with St Bernards and to nailbiters.'

Bryant's 'Save Our Children' campaign succeeded in convincing Florida voters to overturn the ordinance on 7 June 1977 by a two-to-one margin.

She then took her show on the road. One memorable incident captured on film occurred on 14 October 1977 in Des Moines, Iowa, where, during a press conference, Tom Higgins, posing as a journalist, shoved a pie right into Anita's puss. 'Well, at least it's a fruit pie,' she said, and proceeded to pray and ask God to deliver him from his 'deviant lifestyle'.

Ironically, Bryant's campaign energised gay activists around the country, prompting them to organise an orange-juice boycott. One Florida company cashed in by selling Anita Bryant dartboards, so you can 'stick Anita as much as you want for $9.95'.

Bryant's career took a major nosedive in the early 1980s (even the Florida Orange Commission dropped her as their spokeswoman in 1980). Her right-wing Christian supporters also lost interest when she divorced her husband in 1980.

— A COMING OUT STORY —

In the course of her college life, a young woman came to terms with her homosexuality and decided to come out of the closet. Her plan was to tell her mother first, so on her next home visit she went to the kitchen, where her mother was busy stirring the dinner with a wooden spoon. Nervously, she explained to her mother that she had realised she was gay.

Without looking up from her stew, her mother said, 'You mean lesbian?'

'Well…yes. I'm a lesbian.'

Without looking at her, her mother then asks, 'Does that mean you lick women's pussies?'

The young woman stammers, 'Well…yes.'

With that, the mother turns, holds the wooden spoon under her daughter's nose in a threatening manner and snaps, 'Don't you *ever* complain about my cooking again!'

— DEATH BY DROWNING —

In 1568, a young woman in Geneva was charged with fornication with a man. During the trial, she confessed that she had also had sex with a woman four years earlier. Her punishment? She was drowned.

— THE KAPOK DOCTOR —

James Barry was sponsored by the Earl of Buchan to study medicine at Edinburgh University. He graduated at the age of 18 and thereafter worked as an officer and surgeon in the British Army. In 1817, at age 22, Dr Barry was posted to the Cape Peninsula, South Africa, having previously served in Spain, Belgium and India. Only weeks after Barry's arrival, the colonies governor of the time, Lord Charles Somerset, assisted in the doctor's promotion to medical inspector for the colony; saving the life of one of Lord Somerset's daughters did Dr Barry's career no harm at all.

Dr Barry wore three-inch soles on his shoes, dressed effeminately in full dress uniform and cocked hat and had an elaborate set of shoulder pads, said to be the reason for his nickname 'the Kapok Doctor'. He was always seen with a black manservant and a black poodle named Psyche.

Despite his obvious effeminacy, officers were impressed by the doctor's bad temper, which often led to him being sent home under arrest. He wasn't bad-tempered with his patients, however; one woman was reported to say, 'No man could show such sympathy for one in pain.' Dr Barry also saved a baby in what has been purported as the first caesarian section in the English-speaking world; the baby, christened James Barry Munnik, eventually became the godfather to James Barry Munnik Hertzog, later prime minister of South Africa.

Dr Barry cultivated a reputation of being a ladies' man, often flirting with women at army dances, and one of Lord Somerset's daughters was said to have been in love with him. The Lord himself privately commented that Dr Barry was the finest doctor that he had ever seen but 'absurd in everything else'. Even so, he obviously found the doctor entertaining company and often invited him to the Round House, the Lord's shooting box above Camp's Bay. Dr Barry must have enjoyed his time in this area, as it was here and in the surrounding mountains that, according to the late historian Eric Rosenthal, 'the shade of the mysterious Dr "James" Barry has been observed on many occasions'.

Dr Barry left the Cape in 1828, a year after Lord Somerset had returned to England. He was subsequently posted to Mauritius, Trinidad, Saint Helena, Malta, Corfu, the Crimea (where he insulted Florence Nightingale), Jamaica and Canada, eventually reaching the rank of inspector general, HM Army Hospitals. No military doctor could reach a higher rank. In 1864, he retired and returned to England, still with a black manservant and a poodle called Psyche.

In 1865, Dr James Barry died. A doctor signed the death certificate without realising that Dr Barry was a woman, but a charwoman who prepared the body for burial was more observant. It is likely that Dr Barry's manservant, John, was a knowing confidant, having brought her six clean towels every day in order that she could disguise her shape.

Dr Barry's middle name is often given as Miranda, and it is possible that her real name was Miranda Stuart. However, she was buried in Kensal Rise Cemetery, London, as Dr James Barry.

— NOT ALL HOMOSEXUALS ARE ALIKE... —

...and to prove it, here's a list of some of the more familiar labels gay men have applied to one another over the years:

AUNTIE: An older gay man who likes to gossip (usually with other aunties);

CAMP: Someone who is witty, theatrical and over the top – eg, 'Oh, that Arnold, he's such a camp!';

CIRCUIT BOY: A pretty boy who likes to dance and is willing to travel to party – eg, 'Oh, there's goes that circuit boy, Gary, on his way, no doubt, to the White Party!';

CLONE: A gay man who has the same clothes, haircut, etc, as everyone else – eg, 'Oh, that Neil, he's such a West Hollywood clone!';

CLOSET CASE: A gay man who hides and/or denies the fact she's gay;

FEIGELE: Yiddische word for *gay*, usually used in a derogatory manner – eg, 'Oh, my nephew Barry, he's such a *feigele*!';

— NOT ALL HOMOSEXUALS ARE ALIKE... (CONT'D) —

MISS THING: Campy name, usually used in reference to a gay man with an attitude who thinks she's something special – eg, 'Oh, take a look at Miss Thing over there!';

TWINKIE/TWINK: A young, cute gay man with a toned body – who is not the sharpest tool in the shed;

SIZE QUEEN: A gay man who prefers men who are well endowed.

A FEW THINGS TO KNOW ABOUT
— AMELIE MAURESMO —

Here are some pop facts about the first openly lesbian professional tennis player since Martina Navratilova.

BORN: 5 July 1979 in St-Germain-en-Laye, France
RESIDES: Bornel, France
HEIGHT: 5'9" (1.75m)
WEIGHT: 141lb (64.1kg)
PLAYS: Right-handed, with a Dunlop 300G racquet
CLOTHING/SHOES: Nike/Nike Air Zoom Breathe Free
COACH: French Federation Cup coach Loic Courteau
INSPIRATION: Yannick Noah in his 1983 Roland Garros victory

WTA RANKING HISTORY
SEASON ENDING:
  1994: 827
  1995: 290
  1996: 159
  1997: 109
  1998: 29
  1999: 10
  2000: 16
  2001: 9
  2002: 6
  2003: 4
CAREER HIGH SINGLES: 3 (2 February 2004)
CAREER HIGH DOUBLES: 51 (11 December 2000)
LIKES: Go-karting, downhill skiing, horse-riding, listening to Dido, red wine and her golden retriever, Sophia.

— THE BOYS OF BOISE —

In 1955, the sleepy town of Boise, Idaho, was rocked by a scandal involving a local male-prostitution ring that was allegedly operating in and around the city parks and the local YMCA. When the police arrested three men for seducing young boys (who were actually hustlers), an editorial in the *Idaho Daily Statesman* on 3 November 1995, entitled 'Crush The Monster', quoted an unnamed 'responsible court officer' who claimed that the recent arrests only scratched the surface and that 'partial evidence has been gathered showing that several other adults and about 100 boys are involved'. In the following month, *Time* magazine also ran a story on Boise's so-called 'homosexual underworld'. A wave of hysteria swept over Boiseans, who started making false accusations against each other. A curfew for teenagers and kids under 17 went into effect. Adult men became paranoid to the point of being afraid even to congregate in private for a weekly poker game. In the end, over 1,000 men were questioned, but only nine men were arrested and convicted. The subsequent arrests that were made involved adult men engaging in consensual sex.

In his 1965 investigation of the phenomenon, *The Boys Of Boise: Fury, Vice And Folly In An American City*, author John Gerassi revealed that the driving force behind the Boise witch-hunts was a small group of powerful conservatives who were trying to drive a closeted homosexual out of political office.

— THE WHITE, MARMOREAN FLOCK —

Charlotte Cushman (1816–76) was an international celebrity actress who preferred playing strong female roles and parading in breeches on stage to accepting archetypal feminine roles. She was particularly famous for her portrayal of Shakespeare's Romeo. She later set up a 'bachelor household' in around 1870 in Rome with a group of friends and girlfriends that included novelist Matilda Hays and sculptors Anne Whitney, Mary Edmonia Lewis and Emma Stebbins. Some of these were in Boston Marriages. Dubbed by Henry James 'the white, marmorean flock', they created some of the most praised sculptures of their time.

— SARAH WATERS —

Sarah Waters was born in Pembrokeshire, Wales, in 1966 and began writing fiction in 1995, having completed a degree in Canterbury. It was while she was writing her PhD thesis on English and American historical literature that she collected the ideas that have formed the basis for her three successful novels, all of which have been set in Victorian England and contain lesbian characters as their protagonists.

- *Tipping The Velvet* was published in 1998 and has since been adapted and filmed by the BBC.

- In 2000, her second novel, *Affinity*, won the Somerset Maugham Award and was shortlisted for the John Llewellyn Rhys Prize.

- In 2001, she was selected for the Orange Futures promotion and *The Times* Novelist of the Year.

- In 2002, her third novel, *Fingersmith*, was shortlisted for both the prestigious Orange Prize for Fiction and the Man Booker Prize.

- Waters was listed in the Granta 2003 *Best of British Novelists* compilation.

- She is a recipient of the South Bank Award for Literature, 2003, and was named Author of the Year at the 2003 British Book Awards.

— 'A SERIOUS DINING-ROOM TABLE' —

The first mainstream gay-themed TV commercial debuted in March 1994 as part of furniture chain Ikea's new campaign, depicting 'non-traditional families' – including an interracial couple, a divorced mother and parents adopting kids – buying furniture. The ad in question features a middle-aged gay couple, Steve and Mitch, who tell viewers that they've been together for three years and went to Ikea to buy 'a serious dining-room table'. The table they picked out has a leaf, which means, they explain, 'staying together – commitment. We have another leaf waiting for when we really start getting along.'

Donny Deutsch of Deutsch Advertising, which produced the ad, told the *New York Times* that he wasn't concerned about backlash from the religious right because 'the Donald Wildmon fans probably aren't Ikea shoppers in the first place'. The commercial started running on local TV stations in Los Angeles, New York, Philadelphia and Washington on 30 March 1994, but it was pulled when the retailer received a bomb threat.

The commercial opened the closet door for future ads. Here is only a partial list of the products that have used gay-themed ads to hawk their wares and services in national television spots (which can be seen on the web at www.commercialcloset.com):

Bailey's Irish Creme
Calvin Klein Jeans
Chevron
Clothestime
Doritos
Dr Pepper
Federal Express
Heineken
Holiday Inn
Hyundai
John Hancock Financial Services
Levi Strauss & Co
Mercedes–Benz
Miller Lite Beer
Nissan
7-Eleven
Smint
Snapple
Virgin Cola
Volkswagen

— THE DAME IN SPAIN —

The title character of Fernando de Rojas's 1499 Spanish masterpiece *La Celestina* is an old woman whose list of former conquests includes women.

— SOME LESBIAN COMIC HEROES —

NAUGHTY BITS, FEATURING BITCHY BITCH

Roberta Gregory's Bitchy Bitch (who now has a counterpart in Butchy Bitch) has been around since she started appearing in *Naughty Bits*, *a Quarterly Comic Book* published by Fantagraphics Books since 1991. Bitchy is the archetypal bitch who hates everything and everyone and isn't afraid to say so. Check out www.robertagregory.com.

SUBGURLZ

Jennifer Camper's strip *subGURLZ* is about a trio of lesbians living and loving in an abandoned subway.

HOTHEAD PAISAN (HOMICIDAL LESBIAN TERRORIST)

Hothead Paisan is a self-titled Homicidal Lesbian Terrorist. She's ready to take on the world – with a large bazooka! Check out www.marystreet.com/HH.

JANE'S WORLD

Jane and her friends Ethan and Michelle appear in Paige Braddock's *Jane's World* and give a witty running commentary on what it is to be a lesbian in today's world. Check out www.paigebraddock.com.

— TIPPING THE SCALE —

In 1948, sex researcher Dr Alfred Kinsey's groundbreaking study of male sexuality, *Sexual Behavior In The Human Male*, was published. Kinsey and his associates conducted face-to-face interviews with 5,300 white male subjects with some college education about all aspects of their sexuality – what they did, how often they did it and who they did it with (if applicable). According to Kinsey's study…

- 92% of all males reported that they had masturbated;

- 46% of males had engaged in both heterosexual and homosexual activities;

- 37% had at least one same-sex experience to orgasm;

- 4–6% of males were predominantly homosexual between the ages of 16 and 55.

The fact that 37% had had a same-sex experience suggested that homosexual experiences were more commonplace and not limited to a small portion of the population. On the basis of his data, Kinsey reconceived male sexuality as a seven-point-scale continuum with varying degrees of sexual experiences, which also included fantasies, dreams and thoughts.

0   exclusively heterosexual, with no homosexual.

1   predominantly heterosexual, only incidentally homosexual.

2   predominantly heterosexual, but more than incidentally homosexual.

3   equally heterosexual and homosexual.

4   predominantly homosexual, but more than incidentally heterosexual.

5   predominantly homosexual, incidentally heterosexual.

6   exclusively homosexual.

Kinsey's statistics were criticised by some of his colleagues because 25% were prison inmates and 5% were male prostitutes (the rest were volunteers). However, when Paul Gebhard, who succeeded Kinsey as the head of the Kinsey Research Institute, removed the data collected from prison inmates from the sample, there were only minor differences between the results.

— PRESENTING YOUR ONLINE PROFILE —

- Spend a long time thinking about what you want out of a partner, then be specific about it. However, be careful to not be so specific that people whom you might have found attractive self-deselect.

- Have a good picture to include with your profile. Including a picture will increase the number of responses you get by a factor of seven or eight.

- Describe your values, hobbies and, especially, goals in your profile. Avoid sunset-walks-on-a-beach-type descriptions; it doesn't tell the person anything about you except that you lack creativity!

- Keep your profile honest. It won't take long for people to tell if you've exaggerated or lied.

— HOW MANY GAYS AND LESBIANS ARE THERE? —

Estimates range between 3% and 10% of the global population being gay or lesbian, which equates to between 185.5 million and 618.4 million people. If all the gay men and lesbians in the world moved to a single nation state, it would be the third to fifth most populated nation state in the world, out of 192 existing states.

— YOU ARE CORDIALLY INVITED... —

Before same-sex couples were running downtown to the courthouse to get hitched, the following TV couples declared their love in front of millions of viewers – without destroying the sanctity of marriage:

- **2 May 1994** – Ron and Erick on *Northern Exposure*, 'I Feel The Earth Move'

  In this episode, the townspeople of Cicely, Alaska, celebrate the wedding of innkeepers Ron (Doug Ballard) and Erick (Ron R McManus), who almost don't make it down the aisle when they start squabbling over the wedding arrangements. The town's owner, a slightly homophobic ex-astronaut named Maurice Minnifield (Barry Corbin), is the only one who doesn't approve. Ironically, he's the one who in the end convinces Erick to marry Ron, attesting that they seem 'happy as a couple of cuckoo birds'.

  The episode caused quite a controversy when it first aired. Two CBS affiliates, KNOE-TV (Monroe, Louisiana) and WTVT-TV (Dothan, Alabama) chose not to air it and Nestlé pulled out as a sponsor at the last minute. Reverend Donald E Wildmon of the American Family Association also criticised CBS for giving 'the homosexual lifestyle such warm approval'. Even GLAAD wasn't satisfied, as the producers chose not to show Ron and Erick kiss during the ceremony, a decision which – according to producer Diane Frolov – was made because there was a concern that a kiss would distract viewers from the real focus of the episode.

- **12 December 1995** – Leon Carp and Scott on *Roseanne*, 'December Bride'

  To help her business partner, Leon (Martin Mull), and his lover, Scott (Fred Willard), save money on their wedding, Roseanne volunteers to organise the event. When Leon discovers that Roseanne has turned his wedding into a gay circus complete with female impersonators and go-go boys, he's ready to call the whole thing off, but Roseanne finds out what's really going on when he admits to having cold feet.

The guest cast includes June Lockhart as Leon's stuffy mother and comedian Norm Crosby – 'the king of the malaprop' – as the confused Reverend. There are also cameos by Mariel Hemingway – who, a few seasons earlier, played a lesbian who planted a kiss on Roseanne – and an 85-year-old Milton Berle in drag.

• 18 January 1996 – Carol Geller and Susan Bunch on *Friends*, 'The One With The Lesbian Wedding'

Before the friends started to intermarry, they celebrated the wedding of Ross's ex-wife, Carol (Jane Sibbett), and her lover, Susan (Jessica Hecht), in a ceremony officiated at by a minister played by Newt Gingrich's half-sister, Candice. When Carol's dad decides not to participate, Ross decides to walk his ex-wife down the aisle and give her away.

• 4 January 2001 – Joe and Larry on *Will And Grace*, 'Coffee And Commitment'

The wedding of friends Joe (Jerry Levine) and Larry (Tim Bagley) gives a feuding Will and Grace a chance to re-evaluate their friendship and realise that they treat each other more like spouses than friends. Unfortunately, they decide to reconcile in the middle of the ceremony and upstage the nervous couple in the process.

— GAY FOLKS IN THE US —

US research has revealed the following facts concerning children of gays, lesbians and bisexual parents. While this list pertains only to the US, it's probably true for children in other parts of the world.

• Daughters and sons of lesbian, gay and bisexual parents have the same incidence of heterosexuality as the general population.

• Daughters of lesbians have higher self-esteem than daughters of straight women. Sons are more caring and less aggressive.

• There is no evidence to suggest that such children face any more difficulties socialising in school than children of straight parents.

• If they are lesbian, gay or bisexual, they are likely to be much better off than lesbian, gay and bisexual children of straight parents.

• Most 'problems' that daughters and sons of lesbian, gay and bisexual parents are said to have actually stem from going through a divorce, and not their parents' sexual orientation.

• There is no evidence to suggest that children are psychologically or physically harmed by having gay, lesbian or bisexual parents, but evidence exists to suggest that they are not.

— IF THE ANSWER'S LESBIAN, WHAT'S THE QUESTION? —

Q: What does a lesbian take on the second date?
A: A removal van.

Q: What does a lesbian take on the four-year anniversary?
A: A removal van.

Q: What do you call a lesbian who doesn't eat meat?
A: A vagitarian.

Q: If a man and a woman need a marriage licence to get married, what do lesbians need?
A: A liquor licence. (Plus 1,203 marches, 476 lawyers, $3.5 million and an act of government!)

RITA MAE-BROWN: A JUNGLE ROMP
— THROUGH HER ACHIEVEMENTS —

- Born 28 November 1944.

- In the 1960s, she was part of the civil-rights and anti-war movements and helped to start up both the women's movement and the Student Homophile League.

- She participated in the Stonewall Riots ('one of two women, I expect', she says).

- Her first novel was *Rubyfruit Jungle*, about a young girl who is out and accepting of her lesbianism. In 1973, this kind of thinking was revolutionary, but the book continues to sell today and is considered a pioneering lesbian text.

- Her relationships with Martina Navratilova and, later, with Martina's ex, Judy Nelson, have generated thousands of column inches in the gossip papers.

- Fellow author Fannie Flagg (*Fried Green Tomatoes At The Whistle Stop Café*) was a long-term love.

- Mae-Brown has written 16 novels, including the Runymede, Jane Arnold and Sneaky Pie series of books.

- She is also an Emmy-nominated screenwriter and poet.

— GAY DAYS —

You know the times are a-changing when 'gay days' (ie days on which amusement and theme parks extend a special invitation to members of the LGBT community) are held in baseball parks around the US and Canada. Among the professional teams that have sponsored gay days are the Chicago Cubs, the Chicago White Sox, the Philadelphia Phillies, the Toronto Blue Jays, the Texas Rangers, the New York Mets and the Boston Red Sox. Since 1994, the San Francisco Giants have sponsored 'Until There's A Cure', an annual fundraiser for AIDS charities in the community.

— A SHORT LIST OF LESBIAN CHOIRS AND CHORUSES —

Lesbokoor De Heksenketel – Netherlands
The Women Next Door – Canada
Prairie Pride Chorus – Canada
Rainbow Women's Chorus – USA
Deep C Divas – UK
Classical Lesbians – Germany
Sweet and Power – Switzerland
Melodykes – Germany

— HANKY PANKY —

The hanky code is a well-known way for gay males to signal, through the use of a complex relationship of colour to sexual proclivity, what it is they're after for the night. Broadly speaking, if you hang your bandanna or hankie out of your right-hand back pocket, it means you want it done to you, while a hankie hanging from your left-hand back pocket indicates you want to do it to someone. That's the simple bit. Thereafter, the colour coding can make things pretty intricate. It's a code that has also been adopted by lesbians as it's an easy way to advertise your personal preferences without ever having to utter a word.

Lesbian femmes can flag by hanging a scarf off their belt rather than the handkerchief in question. Other common methods of flagging include hanging keys or a pair of handcuffs off of one side. For the uninitiated, here's a list to get you going:

WORN ON LEFT	COLOUR	WORN ON RIGHT
Heavy S&M top	*Black*	Heavy S&M bottom
Bondage top	*Grey*	Bondage bottom
Fister	*Red*	Fistee
Golden-shower top	*Yellow*	Golden-shower bottom
Scat top	*Brown*	Scat bottom
Piercer	*Purple*	Piercee
Anal sex, top	*Dark blue*	Anal sex, bottom
Wants oral sex	*Light blue*	Expert at oral sex
Dildo user, top	*Light pink*	Dildo user, bottom
Likes drag	*Lavender*	In drag
Uniform top	*Olive drab*	Uniform bottom
69er	*Robin's-egg blue*	69er
Breast torturer	*Dark pink*	Breast torturee
Likes menstruating women	*Maroon*	Is menstruating woman

Worn On Left	Colour	Worn On Right
Likes navel worship	*Mauve*	Navel worshipper
2 looking for 1	*Gold*	1 looking for 2
Anything goes	*Orange*	Not now, thanks
Spanker	*Fuschia*	Spankee
Owns a suit	*Grey flannel*	Likes women in suits
Shaver	*Red/white stripes*	Shavee
Starfucker	*Silver lamé*	Star
Bartender	*Cocktail napkin*	Bar groupie
Cuddler	*Teddy bear*	Cuddlee
Gives oil massages	*Handywipe*	Wears it well
Rides a motorcycle	*Chamois*	Likes bikers
Outdoor sex, top	*Mosquito netting*	Outdoor sex, bottom
Lover's out – my place OK?	*Toothbrush*	Your place ONLY

— BEFORE THE PARADE PASSES BY —

One of the New York City police officers who was the first to arrive at the scene on the night of the Stonewall Riots in New York City's Greenwich Village participated in the 2004 New York Gay Pride Parade. Frank Toscano and a fellow retired officer, Richie Orenstein, who was also there on that historic June evening in 1969, reportedly rode in a replica of the squad car that Toscano and his partner Tommy Noble had been riding in that night, licence number RMP 2499 – which is also the title of the screenplay Toscano and Orenstein are reportedly writing about Stonewall from the police's perspective.

— KY —

There isn't a gay-man or lesbian in the Western world who doesn't know what these two letters represent: ease of passage, a smooth ride, no pain but, oh, such gain! This popular lubricant – one of Johnson & Johnson's most successful brands – has been on supermarket shelves for decades and is widely used by men and women to allow easier penetration, particularly of the anus. As a water-based product, it eclipsed other brands from the 1980s when AIDS awareness and the importance of safe sex necessitated the use of condoms, which rot when used with oil-based lubricants, and so KY Jelly sales escalated. If you glance inside the bedside drawers of a gay or lesbian household, you'll most likely find the recognisable white, red and blue tube of this wonderful stuff lurking there.

— US PROFESSIONAL ATHLETES: IN AND OUT —

In a 1976 article that ran in the *Washington Star* as part of a series entitled 'Homosexuality In Sports', ex-professional football player Dave Kopay (San Francisco 49ers, Detroit Lions, Washington Redskins, Green Bay Packers) came out of the closet. Later that year, he revealed in an interview with *The Advocate* that one of the reasons why he came out was because 'younger people need to know the truth, to know that there are successful gay people in every walk of life, including the life of a pro athlete. It would have helped me to know there were others.' Of course, Kopay is not the only gay man to have played professional sports; here's a partial list of gay male athletes and the circumstances around their coming out:

BILLY BEAN

Two years after his retirement from professional baseball, Bean came out publicly on the front page of the *New York Times*. His autobiography, *Going The Other Way: Lessons From A Life In And Out Of Major League Baseball*, was published in 2003.

GLENN BURKE (1952–95)

Burke was a professional baseball player who invented the celebratory 'high five'. He spent a season with the Dodgers, who traded him to the Athletics because he refused to enter a 'marriage of convenience'. Homophobia, combined with a knee injury, shortened his baseball career. He developed a drug problem, spent some time in jail for possession and was severely injured in an automobile accident. He died due to AIDS in 1995. His autobiography, *Out At Home: The Glenn Burke Story*, was published in 1995.

JOHN CURRY (1949–94)

A British Olympic figure skater who came out at a press conference after winning the gold medal at the 1976 Olympic Games, Curry was diagnosed with AIDS in 1991 and died in 1994.

RUDY GALINDO

A Champion figure skater who announced he was gay after winning the US Men's Figure Skating title in 1996. Four years later, he revealed that he was HIV positive in an interview with *USA Today*.

BRUCE HAYES

Ten years after winning a gold medal in the swimming relay at the 1984 Olympics, Hayes was a spokesman and a participant in the Gay Games.

GREG LOUGANIS
The four-time Olympic medal winner (twice in 1984 and again in 1988) also came out at the 1994 Gay Games. The following year, his bestselling autobiography, *Breaking The Surface*, was published and he publicly announced that he had AIDS.

ROY SIMMONS
A former offensive lineman for the Washington Redskins and the New York Giants, Simmons came out in 1992 on Phil Donahue's talk show. In 2003, on World AIDS Day, he went public again and revealed in a *New York Times* interview that he is HIV positive.

'OUT' LESBIAN CHARACTERS IN
— MAINSTREAM COMICS —

Amazon (Marvel)
Amy Chen (Marvel)
Andy Jones (DC)
Annie and Nibble (Eros Comix)
Captain Power (Marvel)
Catatrophe Jen (Marvel)
Closet Space (DC)
Cobweb (ABC)
Donner and Blitzen (Milestone)
Fauna and Syonide (DC)
Flying Fox (Homage)
Hazel and Foxglove (Vertigo)
Holly Robinson (DC)
Jack Phantom (ABC)
Karma (Marvel)
Leather and Lace (Marvel)
Lee and Li (DC)
Lisa (Marvel)
Maggie Sawyer (DC)
Magical Witch Girl Bunny (Slave Labor)
Marisa Rahm (Milestone)
Meg Chancellor (Vertigo)
Melissa Maro (Marvel)
Molly Von Richthofen (Marvel)
Moondragon (Marvel)
Purgatori (Chaos)

'OUT' LESBIAN CHARACTERS IN
— MAINSTREAM COMICS (CONT'D) —

Rebecca Bergier (Marvel)
Rebecca Cross (Marvel)
Sailor Moon (Kodansha/Mixx)
Sihouette (DC)
Sunfire II (Marvel)
Tara Algren and Bethany Flynn (Marvel)
Tristan and Isolde (DC)
Victoria Montesi (Marvel)
Willow and Tara (Dark Horse)

— PFLAG —

PFLAG (Parents and Friends of Lesbians and Gays, www.pflag.org) grew out of a support group formed in 1972 by Jeanne Mumford, a New York City elementary-school teacher and mother of a gay son, Morty. In April 1971, Morty, a Columbia University student, was severely beaten by a firefighter during a demonstration outside the New York Hilton Hotel. When Jeanne and her husband Jules saw the incident on the local news, they were naturally outraged. The following June, Jeanne marched in the Christopher Street Liberation Day parade carrying a sign bearing the legend 'Parents Of Gays: United In Support Of Our Children'. The first meeting of the support group later known as PFLAG was held in a New York City church in March 1973. Headquartered today in Washington, DC, PFLAG has over 200,000 members in 500 communities in the United States and overseas.

— FAMOUS MARRIED LESBIANS —

- Phyllis Lyon and Del Martin (founders of the Daughters of Bilitis)
- Rosie O'Donnell (comedian/actor) and Kelli Carpenter
- Alison Bechdel (cartoonist) and Amy Rubin
- Melissa Etheridge (singer) and Tammy Lynn Michaels
- Janis Ian (singer) and Pat Snyder

— HOMOPHOBIA, USA —

- The majority of victims of anti-lesbian and -gay violence – possibly more than 80% – never report the incident, often due to fear of being 'outed'.

- 85% of teachers oppose integrating lesbian, gay and bisexual themes in their curricula.

- Due to sexual-orientation discrimination, lesbians earn up to 14% less than their heterosexual female peers with similar jobs, education, age and residence.

- More than 84% of Americans oppose employment discrimination on the basis of sexual orientation.

- 75% of people who commit hate crimes are under 30, one in three are under 18, and some of the most pervasive anti-gay violence occurs in schools.

- Lesbian, gay and bisexual youths are four times more likely to commit suicide than their straight peers.

- A 1994 survey of 191 employers revealed that 18% would fire, 27% would refuse to hire and 26% would refuse to promote any person they perceived to be lesbian, gay or bisexual.

— AGE OF CONSENSUS —

Some countries where the ages of consent for lesbians and heterosexuals differ:

COUNTRY	LESBIANS	HETEROSEXUALS
Burkina Faso	21	13
Gabon	21	15
Rwanda	18	16
Albania	18	14
Bulgaria	18	14
Portugal	16	14
Bahamas	18	16
Surinam	18	16

— THE WOMEN OF *THE WOMEN* —

Here's a gay fave, Clare Boothe (Luce)'s play about women with an all-female cast. And here they are, the women of *The Women*:

ROLE	1936 STAGE PRODUCTION	1939 FILM VERSION	1956 MUSICAL (*THE OPPOSITE SEX*)	1973 STAGE REVIVAL	2001 STAGE REVIVAL
Mary, Mrs Stephen Haines	Margalo Gilmore	Norma Shearer	June Allyson (Kay Hilliard)	Kim Hunter	Cynthia Nixon
Crystal Allen	Betty Lawford	Joan Crawford	Joan Collins	Marie Wallace	Jennifer Tilly
Sylvia, Mrs Howard Fowler	Ilka Chase	Rosalind Russell	Dolores Gray	Alexis Smith	Kristen Johnston
Flora, Countess DeLave	Margaret Douglass	Mary Boland	Agnes Moorhead	Jan Miner	Rue McClanahan
Miriam Aarons	Audrey Christie	Paulette Goddard	—	Rhonda Fleming	Lynn Colllins
Edith, Mrs Phelps Potter	Phyllis Povah	Phyllis Povah	Joan Blondell	Dorothy Loudon	Jennifer Coolidge
Peggy, Mrs John Day	Adrienne Marden	Joan Fontaine	—	Marian Hailey	Amy Ryan
Mrs Morehead	Jessie Busely	Lucile Watson	—	Myrna Loy	Mary Louise Wilson
Lucy	Marjorie Main	Marjorie Main	Charlotte Greenwood	Polly Rowles	Julie Halston

- The 1936 stage production of *The Women* premiered on 26 December 1936 at the Ethel Barrymore Theater in New York City. The production was staged by Robert B Sinclair.

- The 1939 film version was directed by George Cukor for MGM.

- The 1956 musical version was directed by David Miller for MGM.

- The 1973 stage revival premiered on 25 April 1973 at the 46th Street Theater. The production was directed by Morton DaCosta.

- The 2001 stage revival premiered on 8 November 2001 at the American Airlines Theater. The production was directed by Scott Elliot.

— KENRIC —

This long-established British lesbian group (1965–present) was formed out of *Arena Three* (1964–71), the first publication in the UK produced by, and for, lesbians. Meetings were started through the magazine, which provided the first forum for London-based lesbians to come together. The name Kenric was derived from Kensington and Richmond, two London boroughs where the original members lived. Generally perceived as the 'nice and normal' face of British lesbianism, the group remains active throughout the country.

— FAR REMOVED FROM REALITY —

In March 2004, Fox Television launched a new reality-TV series entitled *Playing It Straight*. In the show, a female contestant named Jackie, who is looking for Mr Right, travels to a Nevada ranch, where she meets 14 eligible bachelors. But there's a twist: she is told that half the guys are gay, the other half straight. So Jackie and the audience have to switch on their gaydar to separate the heteros from the homos. If she chooses a straight guy, they split $1 million; if he's gay, she gets nothing and he gets all the cash. Only three of the six episodes aired before Fox pulled the plug due to low ratings. However, the episode guide on the network's official website (www.fox.com/playingitstraight/) reveals – if anyone still cares – who Jackie picked and what team he plays on.

Fox must have learned their lesson from this venture, because they also cancelled a two-hour reality-TV special entitled *Seriously, Dude, I'm Gay*, in which straight guys compete for a cash prize by trying to fool people into thinking that they're gay. In a press release dated 27 May 2004, the Gay and Lesbian Alliance Against Defamation (GLAAD) applauded Fox's decision, calling the show 'an exercise in humiliation'. GLAAD also objected to a press release Fox issued earlier that stated, 'It's a heterosexual male's worst nightmare: turning gay overnight.'

PLACES LESBIANS AND GAY MEN CAN
— LEGALLY GET MARRIED —

- In Canada, same-sex couples can marry in Ontario, British Columbia and Quebec.

- The Netherlands has full marriage and registered partnership rights for same-sex or opposite-sex couples.

- France's Civil Solidarity Pact grants same- or opposite-sex partners rights of next of kin, inheritance, social security and tax benefits.

- Portugal grants partnership rights to same- and opposite-sex couples including those of next of kin, inheritance, property, social security and tax benefits.

- In 2003, Belgium became the second country in the world to allow gay and lesbian couples to marry. However, gay and lesbian couples are not allowed to adopt children there.

- In Denmark, same-sex couples can apply for registered partnerships that bestow the same rights as marriage.

- Germany recognises next-of-kin and property-inheritance rights for same-sex couples who register as partners.

- The newly elected Prime Minister of Spain has promised to give same-sex unions the same rights and privileges as heterosexual unions. Jose Luis Rodriguez Zapatero has not set a time when this will happen.

- In 2000, Vermont legislature passed and Governor Howard Dean signed a law creating civil unions for same-sex couples, giving these couples all the rights and benefits of marriage under Vermont law but not marriage licences. Vermont civil unions are recognised only in the states of Vermont and, from 2004, Massachusetts. It is not yet known whether Vermont civil unions will be recognised in California or Oregon.

- On 12 February 2004, San Francisco Mayor Gavin Newsom decided that to deny marriage licences to same-sex couples was discriminatory and against the state's constitution. There followed a frenzied rush of hundreds of gays and lesbians to get married, and on 11 March 2004, the California Supreme Court ordered San Francisco to stop issuing marriage licences.

- Multnomah County, Oregon – which includes Portland – began issuing same-sex marriage licences on 3 March 2004. On 20 April, a judge ordered the county to stop issuing marriage licences to gay and lesbian couples until the State Legislature ruled on the matter. All of the marriages that were performed between 3 March and 20 April are considered legal.

— RUTH AND NAOMI —

In the Old Testament of the Bible, Ruth was the great-grandmother of King David and a direct ancestor of Jesus. The focus of the Book of Ruth is on her loving relationship with Naomi, making it one of the earliest written representations of love between two women. Lesbianism was not forbidden at all in the laws of the time, so there is a very real possibility that this could be as much a story about love as a love story. Ruth is Naomi's daughter-in-law, and when the men are killed Naomi tells both her daughters-in-law to leave and find new lives, as they are still young enough to start again. Orpah leaves but Ruth refuses and begs to stay with Naomi, with the following lines from Ruth 1:16–18:

> 'And Ruth said, Entreat me not to leave thee, or to return
> from following after thee:
> for whither thou goest, I will go;
> and where thou lodgest, I will lodge:
> thy people shall be my people,
> and thy God my God:
> Where thou diest, will I die, and there will I be buried:
> the Lord do so to me, and more also,
> if ought but death part thee and me.
> When she saw that she was steadfastly minded to go with
> her, then she left speaking unto her.'

— DIXIE CHICKS —

In the US in 1863, two passing women serving in the Union Army were discovered when they got drunk and nearly drowned in a Tennessee river. They had enlisted separately and had subsequently, in General Philip Sheridan's words, formed an 'intimacy'. They were discharged from the military, given women's clothing and despatched from the front.

— DILDOS AND ACCESSORIES —

A *dildo* is a vaguely phallus-shaped device used for sexual gratification. They actually come in many different shapes, from very realistic penis shapes to those resembling vegetables, such as corncobs and courgettes, and even dolphins (the non-representational ones are used by lesbians who don't care for phallic shapes).

A *strap-on* is a dildo worn in a harness so that it is situated in the same location as a man's penis would be.

Among lesbians, the term *packing* means wearing a strap-on dildo – usually under clothing – out in public. It can also mean wearing something (such as a pair of rolled-up socks or cotton wool) in the underwear or shorts in order to achieve the illusion that there is something else there.

Usually fashioned from leather, a *harness* is a device that is worn strapped over the hips, crotch or thigh (called a thigh harness) in order to hold a dildo in place for sexual penetration.

— HOW TO CLEAN YOUR SEX TOYS —

- Keep your toys clean with soap and warm water. Hydrogen peroxide can also be used in addition to soap and water.

- Don't submerge the part of a battery-operated vibrator that holds the batteries or any part of an electric vibrator.

- Leather harnesses can be cleaned with a damp rag, and nylon webbing harnesses can go in the wash with the rest of the washing.

- With silicone dildos and butt plugs, boil them for up to three minutes and then clean with a bleach solution, or put them through the dishwasher. For more delicate polymers, warm water and soap are your best bet. These toys should be replaced every now and then, as they are impossible to keep perfectly clean.

- Rubber dildos are porous, so you should either put condoms on them if you're going to use them with multiple people or change to silicone dildos, which can be disinfected by boiling.

- Oil-based lubricants will destroy latex, so be sure to use only water-based products.

- If cleaning isn't your strong suit but you still want to use your toy with more than one partner, latex condoms (or latex gloves for larger vibrators) can be used over your toy and thrown away when you're done.

— THE CURRENT REIGNING QUEENS OF DRAG —

- **Jim Bailey** – Entertainer/comedian with a trained singing voice who is best known for his 'Judy' impersonation.

- **Charles Busch** – Playwright (*Vampire Lesbians of Sodom*, *The Tales Of The Allergist Wife*) who appeared on the big screen in the film versions of his plays *Psycho Beach Party* (2000) and *Die, Mommie, Die* (2003).

- **Dame Edna Everage (Barry Humphries)** – Tony Award-winning dragster who considers herself 'the most popular and gifted woman in the world today'.

- **Jimmy James** – Singer and vocal impersonator whose repertoire includes everyone from Billie to Barbra and Bette to Britney!

- **The 'Lady' Bunny (John Ingle)** – Founder, producer and mistress of ceremonies of the New York dragfest known as 'Wigstock'.

- **Lypsinka (John Epperson)** – Drag star who lip-synchs to a rapid montage of voices of the former grande dames of song and the silver screen.

- **RuPaul (RuPaul Andre Charles)** – A 6'7" drink of water who helped bring drag into the mainstream with his hit record 'Supermodel (You Better Work It)' and talk show.

— UNCONTROLLABLE LUST —

Written in Flanders in around 1200, *The Life Of Saint Godelive* is the story of a martyred 12th-century noblewoman who was later named patroness of Belgium. It briefly mentions that women are naturally prone to almost uncontrollable lusts and that they often satisfy these lusts with one another, especially when sleeping together in the same bed.

— GAY GAMES —

Year	Location	Number Of Sports	Number Of Athletes	Number Of Countries
1982	San Francisco	17	1,350	12
1986	San Francisco	18	3,500	18
1990	Vancouver	27	7,300	27
1994	New York City	31	11,000	40
1998	Amsterdam	34	14,500	(unknown)
2002	Sydney	(unknown)	11,000	70

— LESBIAN BREAST CANCER —

What makes gay women more likely to get breast cancer than their heterosexual sisters?

• Lesbians have the highest concentration of risk factors for this cancer than any subset of women in the world.

  – **Non-maternity** – Risk of breast cancer is reduced by as much as 50% for women who have had a child.

  – **Obesity** – Nearly 30% of lesbians are obese, compared to 20% of women overall.

  – **Alcohol** – Lesbians do not drink more than the general population but have a greater history of problems with alcohol.

  – **Smoking** – Lesbians are more likely to smoke.

• Lesbians are less likely to perform a self-breast examination or get clinical breast examinations or mammograms.

• Lesbians tend to visit their doctors regarding their reproductive health later in life and less frequently than straights, as a result of not requiring birth control or having children, and consequently early-detection pathways are missed.

• Lesbians are less likely to talk to medical professionals about their sexuality (and therefore their gynaecological health) for fear of a homophobic reaction, or simply due to the discomfort of coming out to a stranger.

- Lesbians are less likely to be asked relevant screening questions by healthcare providers because that provider, cognisant of social stigma, feels uncomfortable asking questions (about sexual history) that they feel to be personal.

- Lesbians are less likely to have health insurance, in part due to employers not offering domestic-partner benefits.

THE 10 GREATEST MYTHS ABOUT
— THE MALE HOMOSEXUAL —

1 Male homosexuals are sexually promiscuous by nature and, therefore, want to have sex with all men, gay and straight.

2 Male homosexuals are sexually attracted to young boys.

3 Male homosexuals have a built-in 'gaydar', which they can use to determine instantly another male's sexual orientation.

4 Male homosexuals masturbate more frequently than heterosexual males.

5 The male homosexual is a homosexual because he was raised by an overbearing mother and a distant and/or absent father.

6 The male homosexual is a homosexual because his first heterosexual experience with a woman was traumatic.

7 The male homosexual is a man who, deep down, really wishes he was a woman.

8 The male homosexual is hyper-sexual by nature and is therefore incapable of entering into a long-term monogamous relationship.

9 The male homosexual has inherently good taste and fashion sense.

10 Male homosexuals hate women, particularly lesbians.

— GIRL GUIDES —

In 1889, Paris's *Guide des Plaisirs* told its readers about a Montmartre restaurant frequented by lesbians.

BILLY TIPTON: JAZZ SAXONPHONIST AND
— PASSING WOMAN —

Jazz saxophonist Billy Tipton was a relatively successful musician who toured throughout the Midwest USA during the mid 20th century with such well-known artists as Duke Ellington. He was married five times and was a father to a number of children. However, when he died, it was discovered that he was a woman. Nobody, including his last wife, had known this secret.

Dorothy Lucille Tipton was born in Oklahoma City in 1914. By the age of 19, her parents had split up and she was pursuing a musical career in her home town. She quickly discovered that there were few options for white women in the Depression-era jazz clubs, no matter how talented, so she took a radical step to overcome this obstacle, binding her chest, donning trousers and a hat. Thus Billy Tipton was born.

Tipton toured the US throughout the 1940s and '50s, ending up in Spokane, Washington, where he worked as a booking agent to supplement his small musician's income. He lived there with a woman named Kitty and they adopted three boys. She never knew that Billy was a woman.

Today we have to ask whether we can consider Billy a man or a woman. Altogether five women called themselves Mrs Tipton, and yet not one seemed to know her sexual identity. Clearly his or her sexuality will forever be shrouded in confusion.

— THE REPEAL OF US SODOMY LAWS —

The chart below gives a state-by-state breakdown of sodomy laws in the US. The Supreme Court's 6–3 decision in the 2003 *Lawrence vs Texas* case made the existing sodomy laws that still existed in 14 states unconstitutional (designated with an asterisk).

STATE	YEAR LAW REPEALED
Alabama	2003*
Alaska	1980
Arkansas	2002
Arizona	2001
California	1976
Colorado	1972
Connecticut	1971
Delaware	1973

QUEER FACTS

State	Year law repealed
District of Columbia	1995
Florida	2003*
Georgia	1998
Hawaii	1973
Illinois	1962
Indiana	1977
Iowa	1978
Kansas	2003*
Kentucky	1992
Louisiana	2003*
Maine	1976
Massachusetts	2002
Maryland	1998/1999
Michigan	2003*
Minnesota	2001
Mississippi	2003*
Missouri	2003*
Montana	1997
Nebraska	1978
New Hampshire	1975
New Jersey	1979
New Mexico	1975
New York	1980
Nevada	1993
North Carolina	2003*
North Dakota	1975
Ohio	1974
Oklahoma	2003*
Oregon	1972
Pennsylvania	1980
Puerto Rico	2003*
Rhode Island	1998
South Carolina	2003*
South Dakota	1977
Tennessee	1966
Texas	2003*
Utah	2003*
Vermont	1977
Virginia	2003*
Washington	1976
West Virginia	1976
Wisconsin	1983
Wyoming	1977

197

— CRUISING TO THE NEWS —

Closeted lesbians in professional women's sport have probably been around for as long as professional women's sport itself, but numerous athletes have had to hide their romantic choices in order to protect their global marketability and the financial reward that this breeds.

The corporate world has historically had reservations when faced with a 'known' lesbian representing their brand or product. Despite the open secret that many sportswomen in, for example, the tennis and golf world are lesbians, how many have secured sponsorship deals where the sponsor has encouraged a public declaration of their lesbianism? The answer to this question was probably none, until March 2004, when American professional golfer Rosie Jones became the face of Olivia Cruise Lines, a travel company providing all-women cruises around America and its neighbouring countries. During her successful 21 years as a professional golfer, Rosie Jones's sexuality was an open secret, but in the publishing of her column 'First, A Word About Me And My Sponsor' in the *New York Times*, the 'secret' was no more. Rosie Jones was never in the closet, but she had finally chosen to go public, and her sponsor didn't mind a bit!

— I'M NOT GAY. I'M NOT EVEN REAL. —

No one can hide from the fickle finger of homophobia – not even these fictional characters who have been accused of committing 'crimes against nature':

- In 1993, a booklet entitled 'The Purple Messiah' by Reverend Joseph Chambers, a Free Pentecostal Pastor, accused Barney, the large purple dinosaur, of being a cult leader who educates children about diversity, which Chambers equates with homosexuality.

- In 1994, Reverend Chambers tried to get *Sesame Street*'s Bert and Ernie banned, claiming, 'They are two grown men sharing a house and a bedroom. They share clothes, eat and cook together, and have blatantly feminine characteristics.' The show's producers, the Children's Television Workshop, had released statements in the past explaining that Bert and

Ernie 'do not portray a gay couple, and there are no plans for them to do so in the future. Like all the Muppets created for *Sesame Street*, they were designed to help educate pre-schoolers. Bert and Ernie are characters who help demonstrate to children that, despite their differences, they can be good friends.'

• In the February 1999 issue of the *National Liberty Journal*, Moral Majority founder Reverend Jerry Falwell warned parents about Tinky-Winky, the purple Teletubby, because there are some clear signs that he is gay. As evidence, Falwell submits the fact he's a boy (his voice is male), he carries a smart red handbag (actually a 'magic bag'), he is purple and he has a triangle on his head, both of which are symbols of gay pride. Falwell did not comment on the sexual orientation of Tinky-Winky's fellow Tubbies Dipsy, Po and Laa-Laa.

— TOP OF THE OSCARS —

Costume designer Edith Head has been nominated for more Oscars than any other person in history, with 8 wins and 35 nominations in all for over 1,100 films. She worked Hollywood's studio system from the Silent Era through the Golden Era until her death in 1981. Bette Davis, Grace Kelly, Elizabeth Taylor, Audrey Hepburn, Gloria Swanson, Ginger Rogers, Veronica Lake, Shirley MacLaine and Ingrid Bergman are among the acclaimed list of artists who were dressed by this superstar. Oscars were awarded for *The Heiress* (1949), *All About Eve* and *Samson And Delilah* (both 1950, the only year in which one designer received awards for costume design in both colour and black-and-white movies), *A Place In The Sun* (1951), *Roman Holiday* (1954), *Sabrina* (1955), *The Facts Of Life* (1960) and *The Sting* (1974). She was married to production designer Wiard Ihnen for 30 years, but it was widely rumoured, with her bespectacled mannish looks and her Greta Garbo fascination, that Edith Head was a lesbian.

— JAPANESE LESBIANISM —

In 1686, Japanese author Ihara Saikaku's *The Life Of An Amorous Woman* included a brief account of sex between the book's heroine and a female employer. Nearly 100 years later, in around 1785, popular prints by Kitagawa Utamaro and other artists depicted erotic encounters between women.

— DYKE TYPES —

CHAPSTICK LESBIAN: A lesbian who is very into sports; a sporty dyke.

FEMME/FEM: A feminine woman, usually a lesbian.

LEATHERDYKE: A lesbian who is a member of the leather/BDSM community.

LIPSTICK LESBIAN: A lesbian who behaves in a very feminine manner or wears a lot of make-up.

LOW FEMME: A femme lesbian who is not quite as stereotypically feminine as a High Femme.

HIGH FEMME: A very, very feminine-acting person.

STONE FEMME: 1. A femme lesbian who never tries to convert her stone-butch lover but instead prefers to pleasure her lover by taking a passive role in sex.
2. A femme lesbian who does not like to be touched.

GLAMOUR BUTCH: A butch who likes to wear fancy clothes.

CLONES: Any group of gay men or lesbians who dress alike and have similar interests, such as flannel-shirt dykes.

DYKON: A lesbian icon, such as kd lang, Melissa Etheridge or Ellen DeGeneres.

EARTHY-CRUNCHY DYKE: A lesbian who is usually vegetarian and usually either New Age or Neopagan and has a tendency to change her name to something like Sparrow – as in Alison Bechdel's *Dykes To Watch Out For* – or Lavender CrystalPower.

PC (POLITICALLY CORRECT) DYKE: A lesbian who is very careful in her language not to offend those people who are currently the pet minorities.

GOLD-STAR LESBIAN: A lesbian who never has had and never intends to have sex with a man. Sometimes they also get points for never sleeping with bisexuals.

DRAG KING: A woman dressed like a man.

LUPPIES: Lesbian urban professionals, or lesbian yuppies.

SATURDAY-NIGHT BUTCH: A term from the 1950s and '60s that means that the butch is dressed as such only at the weekends.

SOFT BUTCH: A butch lesbian who is not as hardcore as a Stone Butch.

STONE BUTCH: A very masculine-acting woman. The term is said to come from African–American slang, in which *stone* means 'very'.

SWITCH: One who is both a top and a bottom, in the leather sense, and switches back and forth, or someone who is sometimes butch, sometimes femme and sometimes androgynous.

DADDY: A more butch, older or experienced lesbian in a relationship with a mama or a 'boy' (usually also a lesbian).

BITCH: A femme submissive.

BOY: A boyish butch lesbian.

DOMME/DOMINATRIX: Someone who enjoys dominating another person in a domination-and-submission scene. A dom may or may not be a sadist. The term *dom* is masculine, while *domme* and *dominatrix* are feminine.

— MARGUERITE YOURCENAR —

Marguerite Yourcenar (1903–87) was a Belgian-born French novelist, short-story writer, essayist and poet who wrote under the pseudonym De Crayencour. Elected to the Académie Française in 1980, she was the first woman to be so honoured. Her published output began in 1921 and was of a consistently high quality, and she lived for many years in the US with her female lover of 42 years. She is famous for writing about the gay-male experience, and today her books are considered to be classics of gay-male fiction.

— AN EXECUTIVE ORDER —

In 1950, at the height of the Red Scare, a US Senate subcommittee named Employment of Homosexuals and Other Sex Perverts in the US Government stated that the US government should not employ homosexuals because they...

* 'violate the laws or the accepted standards of morality';

* are susceptible to blackmailers because of 'their lack of emotional stability...and the weakness of their moral fiber';

* tend to surround themselves with other homosexuals, so if they are in a position of power, they will place other homosexuals in government jobs.

The report also stated that 1,700 applicants for federal positions were denied employment between 1 January 1947 and 1 August 1950 because they had a record of homosexuality or other 'sex perversion'. During that same period, 207 government employees were fired and 213 resigned for similar reasons. The subcommittee concluded that 'it is in the public interest to get sex perverts out of Government and keep them out', yet it must be 'carried out in a manner consistent with the traditional American concepts of justice and fair play'.

Three years later, President Dwight D Eisenhower took matters into his own hands and signed Executive Order 10450 – 'The Loyalty and Security Program' – which made homosexuality legal grounds for exclusion for federal employees. The law wasn't revised until 1995, when President Bill Clinton signed an Executive Order on 4 August 1995 barring the federal government from denying security clearances to homosexuals.

WHAT NOT TO DO IN A
— LESBIAN INTERNET CHATROOM —

DO NOT...
* Trust anyone who takes less than 30 seconds for a loo break. Even if they're sitting right next to a toilet, it'll take a chick longer than that to get her kit off and on again.

* Have a conversation with anyone who begins with 'I'm a woman, are you?' Any person who needs to announce their gender probably isn't what they claim to be.

- Trust anyone who asks for your bra size. How many lesbians do you know who would ask that straight up?

- Trust someone who brags that they can remove your bra in just under a minute. Dykes can pull this feat off with only a flick of the fingers; what's going on for the other 50 seconds?

- Enter a chat room where the topic is 'All Lesbians! Men Welcome! – Channel for lesbians and the men who love them.' This is NOT the place you want to be!

- Trust anyone who gets the spelling of lesbian or dyke wrong. If they don't know whether they're a woman or a kind of dam, do you really want to talk to them?

- Have cyber sex with anyone who begins by asking, 'OK then, where do I start?' If an anatomy lesson is necessary, they probably haven't got the same bits as you.

- Give someone your phone number if they tell you that they can get it whether you give it to them or not. That sort of threat can't be a good sign!

— RADICAL WOMEN —

In 1912, the women's group Heterodoxy was formed in New York City, riding the wavefront of America's growing women's movement at that time. Shortly afterwards, in 1915, while on a speaking tour across the US, Emma Goldman defended homosexuality together with free love, birth control and pacifism. On a separate speaking tour on 4 February 1915 in Chicago, Edith Lees Ellis – the openly lesbian wife of Havelock Ellis – challenged women to begin 'organising a new love world'. Within weeks, Margaret Anderson's *Little Review* (whose foreign editor was Ezra Pound and which later published James Joyce's *Ulysses* in instalments), which she edited with her lover Jane Heap, chastised Edith Lees Ellis for the timidness of her pro-lesbian remarks. Her article is probably the first justification of same-sex love published by an American lesbian.

— THEY'RE GAY (AND THEY'RE DRAWN THAT WAY) —

Here's a list of some bisexual and gay comic-book and comic-strip characters:

• *Harry Chess – The Man From A.U.N.T.I.E.*: This gay James Bond-type hero created by Al Shapiro appeared in *Drum* magazine in the mid 1960s. Harry also had a gay sidekick, Mickey Muscle.

• *Miss Thing*: Campy strip created by Joe Johnson featuring a stereotypical limp-wristed fairy. Miss Thing appeared in *The Advocate* in the late 1960s/early 1970s.

• **Eric (Brown Bomber) Gambrell:** A 19-year-old African–American gay superhero created by Rupert Kinnard. The character first appeared in Kinnard's college newspaper and then ran in the Portland, Oregon, gay newspaper *Just Out*.

• *Doonesbury*'s **Andy Lippincott and Mark Slackmeyer:** In 1976, law student Joanie Caucus fell in love with Andy Lippincott at law school; he told her he was gay on 10 February 1976. Andy has AIDS when he returns in 1989. He dies while listening to The Beach Boy's 'Wouldn't It Be Nice'. His last words are 'Brian Wilson is God.'

Andy reappeared in 1993 in Mark Slackmeyer's dream to help the ex-college radical come out of the closet.

• *Life In Hell:* Strip by Matt Groening featuring Akbar and Jeff, a gay couple who wear matching fezes, shorts and a Charlie Brown-style shirt. In 1986, they are asked 'How come your people took a perfectly normal word – "gay" – and ruined it for the rest of us?' 'Because we *are* gay!' they declare in unison. In that same year they went to a gay bar, where all the patrons looked like them.

The strip also addressed the 1986 US Supreme Court sodomy ruling ('Damn the law!') as well as the issues of getting an HIV test (1989) and testing positive (1991).

• **Wendel:** The trials and tribulations of this gay character, created by Howard Cruse, appeared in *The Advocate* from 1983 to 1989.

• **Extraño:** The first gay superhero was an effeminate gay Hispanic man who appeared in DC Comics' *Millennium* in 1988.

- **Northstar:** After ten years on the scene, Marvel Comics' superhero Northstar came out of the closet in 1992.

- **Laurence Poirier:** A gay teenager in Lynn Johnston's daily strip *For Better Or Worse* who comes out to his family in 1993 and is thrown out of the house. Five of the 1,400 newspapers that carry the strip refused to run it. In June 1994, Andy took his boyfriend to his high-school prom.

- **The Rawhide Kid:** This red-haired gay cowboy, created by *The Howard Stern Show* scribe Ron Zimmerman, rode into town in February 2003.

— WOMEN'S DOUBLES —

Dating from the end of the Upper Paleolithic Era (c12,000BC), there is evidence of human works of art, such as cave paintings, which indicate that perhaps homosexuality isn't a modern invention. Included among these are supposedly phallic 'batons', one of which is a carved double dildo from the Gorge d'Enfer in present-day France that seems to have been devised for two women to use together.

— THE BEST OF WEST —

Classic lines written and spoken by the immortal Mae West (1893–1980):

'I've been in more laps than a napkin.'

'When I'm good, I'm good. When I'm bad, I'm very good.'

'Those who are easily shocked should be shocked more often.'

'It's not the men in my life that counts, it's the life in my men.'

'A hard man is good to find.'

'Men are my life; diamonds are my career!'

'I generally avoid temptation unless I can't resist it.'

'You're never too old to become younger.'

'Too much of a good thing can be wonderful.'

— THE DILDO HARNESS – ONE STRAP OR TWO? —

Harnesses come in two basic styles: one strap or two. Which sort do you want and how do you choose? If you're a 'strap-on virgin', your best bet is to ask yourself whether you feel better in a G-string or a jock-strap? Allow your answer to guide your decision, but here are the pros and cons of each:

SINGLE STRAP
- Fits like a G-string
- Easy to take on and off
- Middle strap is not adjustable (so smaller women can find it too long)
- O-ring is permanent in most models
- Dildo makes contact directly with your skin rather than against a pad
- Dildos with balls can be bulky and look awkward
- Wearer can achieve clitoral stimulation via the middle strap

DOUBLE STRAP
- Two leg straps fit around your buttock crease, where your butt meets your thigh
- Snug and secure fit
- This style is generally felt to give better control over the dildo
- Pudendum is protected from the dildo by padded material
- Straps are adjustable so most women can find one to fit
- Wearer's vulva and anus aren't covered by the harness material
- Easier to wear for longer periods of time
- Some varieties offer snap-out O-rings so different-sized dildos can be accommodated

Once you've made your stylistic choice, there's the fabric type to consider. Should you get leather, vinyl, rubber or nylon? Buckles or D-rings? Adjustable O-ring? Bullet vibe or not? It's a purchasing decision that can't be taken lightly, so research your subject matter well. And remember, girls, to give yourself a little extra time to decide on the colour!

— FIRST LESBIAN POETRY IN RUSSIA —

In 1916, the first Russian poetry written in an openly lesbian voice was published. *Poems*, Sophia Parnok's anthology of love poetry, is addressed to the poet Marina Tsvetaeva, her lover.

— IT'S IN THE STARS —

In around AD50 in the Roman Empire, Dorotheos of Sidon was one of several astrologers who made reference to birth charts that caused both men and women to experience sexual attraction for members of the same sex.

— CLIPPING THE RIGHT WING —

Over the past ten years, the religious right in America have become increasingly vocal in their opposition to the gay-rights movement. They are also becoming easier to spot. Note how many have the words 'American' and/or 'Family' in their names.

- **The American Family Association** – An organisation founded by Reverend Don Wildmon that represents and stands (according to their website) for 'traditional family values, focusing primarily on the influence of television and other media – including pornography – on our society'. Their website also answers the question that's on everyone's mind: 'Does AFA hate homosexuals? Absolutely not! The same Holy Bible that calls us to reject sin calls us to love our neighbor. It is that love that motivates us to expose the misrepresentation of the radical homosexual agenda and stop its spread through our culture!'

- **Focus On The Family** – An Evangelical Christian group founded by Dr James Dobson that 'supports the teaching of traditional family values as expressed in the historic Christian faith'. In addition to homosexuality, they oppose abortion, pornography and 'juvenile sexual behavior'.

- **Family Research Council** – An organisation devoted to 'defending family, faith and freedom' by 'championing marriage and family as the foundation of civilisation, the seedbed of virtue and the wellspring of society'.

- **The American Cause** – Founded in 1993 by Patrick Buchanan, the American Cause's mission is to 'advance and promote traditional American values'.

— AUSTRIA OUTLAWS LESBIANISM —

In 1852, Austria made sex between women illegal for the first time.

— HONOURABLE DISCHARGE —

Deborah Sampson was honourably discharged from the Massachusetts Regiment on 25 October 1783 in West Point, New York, after being wounded in one of a number of battles in which she had fought. She had kept her gender secret for almost a year and a half until she fell ill with a fever, making her one of the earliest American examples of a passing woman. Sampson had several relationships with women while dressed as a man but later married and took a military pension.

— THE COST OF AN EDUCATION —

In early 2004, 18-year-old UK lesbian Rosie Reid put an ad on eBay, auctioning her 'virginity' to the highest bidding man in order to raise the money required to pay her university fees. The highest bidder, a 44-year-old Londoner, paid £8,400 for the experience.

— GAY MEDIA TASK FORCE PLATFORM —

In the 1970s, the Gay Media Task Force served the dual role of watchdog and consultant for the American mass media to ensure that gay men and lesbians were being represented fairly and accurately on television and in films. The Task Force's platform, which reads like a list of dos and don'ts, was adopted in 1973 and distributed to network executives, TV writers and producers.

GAY MEDIA TASK FORCE PLATFORM
- Homosexuality isn't funny. Sometimes, of course, anything can be a source of humour, but the lives of 20,000,000 Americans are not a joke.

- Fag, faggot, dyke, queer, lezzie, homo, fairy, mary, pansy, sissy, etc, are terms of abuse. If you don't want to insult, the words are gay, lesbian and homosexual. This doesn't mean that nobody on film can use a dirty word, but if you have general rules about the use of kike, wop, spic and nigger, use them for dyke, fag, *et al*.

- Use the same rules you have for other minorities. For example, if bigots don't usually get away with it if they hate Catholics, they can't get away with it if they hate gays. To put it another way, the rights and dignities of homosexuals are not a 'controversial' issue.

- Stereotypical people do exist, but if such a minority of any group receives exclusive media exposure, that's bigotry. Until a broad spectrum of the gay community has been portrayed on film, and the stereotypes are put in perspective, the use of stereotypes is damaging.

- Homosexuality is a natural variant of human sexuality. It is not an illness, nor is it a 'problem' for the vast majority of gays who are pleased and happy to be what they are. If all blacks (or Jews, or Irish, Chicanos, etc) were presented as anguished, oddball or insane, blacks (etc) would be angry. Gays are angry.

- If you are doing a drama, a comedy, a talk show or whatever about homosexuality or gay characters, you have an obligation to do your homework and to free yourself of the myths.

- There is a wide variety of available themes concerning the place of homosexuality in contemporary society and the range of gay relationships and lifestyles, and many of these can provide viable entertainment for a broad public. Gay people do not want to return to media invisibility.

- A permanent board of consultants, consisting of gay women and men (including knowledgeable professionals in a variety of fields), is now available to the industry. But there are gay people all around you in your job. It's up to you to provide the climate in which they feel free to speak out.

— RIVER OF THE AMAZONS —

The early Portuguese explorers of Brazil named the river they discovered there the 'River of the Amazons' after the female warriors of the Tupinamba Indians that they found there. This harked back to their own knowledge of an earlier race of powerful women, the Amazons.

Early missionaries wrote of the relationships these women formed with each other, which even allowed women to take wives and carry weapons. It was clearly not a situation the Portuguese colonial authorities were going to accept, and by 1646 they had extended the laws forbidding same-sex relations to include women as well as men, with burning at the stake as the punishment. While the women may no longer exist, the name of the river endures as a reminder.

— WHAT IS KOROPHILIA? —

The lesbian version of paedophilia, korophilia is a term used to describe the erotic attraction of an adult woman for a young girl. It derives from the Greek word for young girl and is often interchanged with another term, *parthenophilia*, which stems from the Greek word *parthenos*, meaning 'virgin'. Both words were probably created by German gay activist Magnus Hirschfield to delineate different forms of lesbian attraction.

— LESBIAN SEPARATISM —

Lesbian separatism grew out of the conviction that the lesbian political agenda could never be satisfied while lesbians were co-aligned with men and male dominance. Its manifestation in lesbian politics runs the full spectrum, from the belief in women-only spaces right through to the belief that women should completely disassociate themselves from men and all things male. It is very much a product of the growth of lesbian political consciousness and feminism in the early 1970s and has a long association with other ideals, such as vegetarianism, leftist politics, gaia theory, etc.

By April 1970, women in New York City were sufficiently disillusioned with the male dominance of most gay social events to organise the first women-only dances. These were followed shortly, on 1 May 1970, by a group of women protesting against anti-lesbian sentiment in the women's movement at the Second Congress to Unite Women, also in New York City. At the same Congress, radical lesbians distributed the tract 'Woman-Identified Woman', which advocated lesbianism as a political choice and solidarity with separatism.

By the late summer of 1970, women active in the Gay Liberation Front had formed a subgroup, the Gay Women's Liberation Front, which later broke away to start an independent organisation: Gay Liberation Front Women. In October 1970, police raided and harassed a private meeting of the Daughters of Bilitis and many members of this largely non-activist movement began to believe that there was a compelling argument for increasing the militancy of the lesbian movement.

By early 1971, Ti-Grace Atkinson was advocating *political lesbianism*, a total and exclusive commitment to women that may or may not include sex, and lesbian newspaper *The Spectre* was publishing one of the earliest position statements of lesbian separatism.

The movement was quick to gather global support, and by September 1971, lesbian separatism in the Netherlands had led to the establishment of the all-women's group Lavender September. It didn't take long for the backlash to happen, however, and by 4 March 1973, Betty Friedan, one of the founders of the National Organisation for Women, was telling the *New York Times* that 'man-hating' lesbians were trying to take control of the organisation.

Later that same year, *Dykes And Gorgons* – a publication of the East Coast-based Gutter Dyke Collective – called upon lesbians to 'rid the world of men', the first step being that 'wimmin' must stop having male babies. This radical stance angered and alienated many women and many hitherto supporters of lesbian political movements. The collective was also one of the first to declare that male-to-female transsexuals cannot be lesbians, an issue that is still controversial today.

— DOMAIN DIVERSITY —

It is now possible to obtain internet domain names ending in the suffixes .gay and .lesbian.

— THE TABOO ON SAPPHIC ROLES IS BROKEN —

Or so it appears. With an influx of lesbian characters being written for the screen, directors, producers and casting professionals are inundated with female actors vying for the parts. This sees a change from days gone by, when playing a lesbian character was considered by most as the definitive career-stopper. Recent sapphic roles have been played by some big Hollywood names:

Hilary Swank..*Boys Don't Cry*
Salma Hayek..*Frida*
Charlize Theron and Christina Ricci ....*Monster*
Gina Gershon and Lori Petty......................*Prey For Rock 'n' Roll*
Frances McDormand and Kate Beckinsale ....*Laurel Canyon*
Meryl Streep, Julianne Moore, Nicole Kidman and
     Allison Janney...*The Hours*
Heather Graham and Saffron Burrows ....*Gray Matters*
Monica Belluci and Ling Bai......................................*She Hate Me*
Kelly Preston and Famke Janssen ....*Eulogy*

— EACH AND EVERY ONE A VIRGIN —

By today's standards, some of our more illustrious gay writers would be considered late bloomers when it comes to sex:

• André Gide was 23 when he lost his virginity to an Arab Tunisian boy on a sand dune.

• Tennessee Williams lost his in New Orleans to a paratrooper when he was 28.

• EM Forster had already published three novels before he had his first sexual experience, with a 31-year-old man.

• Oscar Wilde was 32 and married before he experienced the love that dare not speak its name.

— THE FIRST AUSTRALIAN LESBIAN ORGANISATION —

In January 1970, a group of women in Melbourne founded a local branch of the Daughters of Bilitis, which became the first gay or lesbian organisation in Australia. By July, they began to hold public meetings, with a straight woman acting as spokesperson for the group. Shortly afterwards, on 8 October 1971, Australia was ready for its first public gay and lesbian rights demonstration in Sydney, held outside the headquarters of the Liberal Party. Gay writer and activist Dennis Altman was one of about 70 protesters.

— MALE MASTURBATION EUPHEMISMS — INVOLVING FOOD

Banging your bacon
Banging the burrito
Basting the ham
Beating the bologna
Beating the butter
Beating your meat
Beef-stroke-it-off

Bludgeoning the beefsteak
Buffing the banana
Buttering the corn
Calling down for more mayo
Cheese off
Chilling the dill
Choking the chicken
Clubbing the ham
Creaming the banana
Cuffing the carrot
Doodling your noodle
Jerking your beef
Juicing the banana
Kneading the bread
Making instant pudding
Making a fist sandwich
Making the bread rise
Mustard on the burger
Paddling the pickle
Peeling the banana
Playing with your noodle
Pulling the pudding
Pulling your taffy
Rocking the rhubarb
Seasoning your meat
Shaking the sausage
Slamming the ham
Slapping the salami
Slinging the jelly
Smoking the bratwurst
Snapping the radish
Squeezing the juice
Stirring the soup
Straining your cabbage
Stroking your twinkie
Tenderising the meat
Tickling the taco
Toasting the marshmallow
Tuffing the tubesteak

— HANDBALLING HOUSEHOLD —

Lesbian couple Camilla Andersen of Denmark and
Norwegian Mia Hundvin, who legally married in Denmark,
became the first spouses to play each other in Olympic
competition, when Denmark and Norway played in the
first round of the handball competition at the Sydney
Olympics in 2000. Denmark went on to win gold and
Norway the bronze medal. Andersen and Hundvin have
since divorced.

— THE L WORD —

This glossy, groundbreaking show, written and produced by Ilene Chaiken,
is the first *bona fide* lesbian soap opera, devoted to the lives and loves of a
cast full of gorgeous dykes. The L in the title is said to stand for ladies, love,
Los Angeles and, most importantly, you know what! Likened by one of its
stars to *Sex And The City*, or at least how that show would be 'if the girls
slept with each other', the series has been promoted with the catchy strap
line 'same sex, different city'. It premiered in the States on cable channel
Showtime in January 2004 and on Channel Seven in Australia on 31 March
of that year, while British viewers had to wait until September before Living
TV aired the first episode there.

THE MAIN CHARACTERS

CHARACTER	ACTOR	
Jenny Schecter	Mia Kirshner	Gifted young fiction writer who moves to LA to be with her boyfriend but whose world is unexpectedly rocked by female attraction
Tim Haspel	Eric Mabius	Jenny's soon-to-be fiancé, who coaches swimming at the university
Bette Porter	Jennifer Beales	Museum curator who wants to have a baby with Tina, her girlfriend of seven years, despite signs of their relationship floundering
Tina Kennard	Laurel Holloman	Bette's girlfriend who has quit her job as a movie executive in order to get pregnant

CHARACTER	ACTOR	
Kit Porter	Pam Grier	Bette's straight half-sister, a recovering alcoholic, musician, singer and club owner
Marina Ferrer	Karina Lombard	Jenny's 'affair' and owner of the LA coffee shop where all the girls go to hang out
Alice Pieszecki	Leisha Hailey (an 'out' lesbian)	Dippy bisexual journalist who hasn't had much luck finding that special someone
Shane McCutcheon	Katherine Moennig	Sultry resident hairdresser and heart-throb, she plays-the-field with a list of women
Dana Fairbanks	Erin Daniels	Professional tennis player and coach, not yet out of the closet and trying to keep it that way

— LESBIAN VAMPIRES —

Vampires have featured commonly in horror films since the genre began. Arguably based on an early belief in the predatory nature of lesbians, the female characters in these movies have often been portrayed as women lusting after weaker and more helpless women. Perhaps the first lesbian vampire appeared in *Dracula's Daughter* (1936), in which the Countess Alesca covertly seduces her weaker victim.

Comparably explicit lesbian scenes didn't return until Roger Vadim's *Blood And Roses* appeared in 1960. Meanwhile, 1971's *Vampyros Lesbos* – considered a classic in the genre – and the English *Lust For A Vampire* both had strong lesbian content.

Later lesbian vampire films have included *Blood-Spattered Bride* (1972), Joseph Larraz's *Vampyres* (1974), *Because The Dawn* (1988), *Carmilla* (1990), *Caress Of The Vampire* (1996) and *Hot Vampire Nights* (2000). Perceived by some to be a sign of society's evolving tolerances, lesbian vampires of the modern day are becoming nicer characters.

— CROSSING GENERATIONAL LINES —

Some of the most provocative gay films of the post-Stonewall era have been
inter-generational love stories involving an adult male who falls in love with
a younger male or teenager. Although their relationship is consensual, such
a relationship remains one of society's greatest taboos. Consequently, many
of these films have tragic endings.

ABUSE (1983, US, DIR ARTHUR BRESSAN)
LARRY (Richard Ryder), a 35-year-old filmmaker who is shooting a
documentary about child abuse

– and –

THOMAS (Raphael Sbarge), one of his subjects, who is being abused by his
parents.

THE CONSEQUENCE (1977, WEST GERMANY, DIR WOLFGANG PETERSEN)
MARTIN (Jürgen Prochnow), a gay actor who has been imprisoned for
seducing a minor

– and –

THOMAS (Ernst Hannawald), the prison warden's teenage son.

THE DEPUTY (1978, SPAIN, DIR ELOY DE LA IGLESIA)
ROBERTO (José Sacristán), a left-wing, up-and-coming, closeted congressman

– and –

JUANITO (José Luis Alonso), a young hustler who has been hired by fascists
to kill Roberto.

ERNESTO (1979, ITALY, DIR SALVATORE SAMPIERI)
A nameless day labourer (Michele Placido)

– and –

Ernesto (Martin Halm), a bourgeois Italian/Jewish teenager.

FOR A LOST SOLDIER (1993, NETHERLANDS, DIR ROELAND KERBOSCH)
WALT (Andrew Kelley), a Canadian soldier stationed in the Netherlands in
World War II

– and –

JEROEN (Maarten Smit), a teenager from the city sent to live on a farm.

— 'OUT' GOLFING GIRLS —

Whether by their own choice or not, these professional golfers have been publicly outed:

Karrie Webb (Australia)
Kelly Robbins (USA)
Rosie Jones (USA)
Muffin Spencer-Devlin (USA)
Patty Sheehan (USA)

— BUFFY THE VAMPIRE SLAYER —

Over the seven years of its existence, *Buffy* (as it is known amongst the cognoscenti) almost single-handedly redefined lesbian representation on mainstream television.

As a result of the lesbianisation of Alyson Hannigan's character, Willow – who starts the series off straight, does not pass bisexuality but goes straight to lesbianism without collecting her 200 smackeroos *en route* (oft cited as a somewhat unrealistic portrayal) – and her first girlfriend, Tara (Amber Benson), this series has seen a number of firsts for popular TV.

The series began in 1997 and ran through until the end of 2003, and Willow was a central character in all seven seasons. A lesbian character from the fourth season on, she appeared in almost all of the 144 episodes and has an enduring popularity amongst fans. Willow and Tara's relationship lasted two and a half years, making it the longest lasting lesbian relationship ever on TV. In the episode 'Seeing Red', they were shown naked together in bed, post-sex, exhibiting a type of lesbian intimacy never before seen on mainstream TV. Later, the show challenged this even further when Willow and Kennedy appeared in the first lesbian sex scene ever on mainstream TV (not just kissing, or hinting, but full-on sex) in the episode 'Touched'.

Kennedy came along after Tara's death and set some of her own lesbian records. She was only the second regular Latina lesbian character on TV (the first being Lisa Vidal's character on ER) but was really the first lesbian action hero on TV.

Buffy is truly a frontrunner not only of the vampire genre but also in redefining televisual representation of lesbians and making a space for them on the small screen.

— LESBIAN HAIRSTYLES —

- THE ETON CROP: Short hairstyle popular in the 1920s and '30s. Essential part of the butch image of Radclyffe Hall (see page 78), who had become the public face of lesbianism in the UK at that time.

- THE MULLET: Late 1970s and early '80s – needs no introduction!

- THE TAIL: Early 1980s.

- THE BALD HEAD: Mid-late 1990s.

- THE PORCUPINE: Popularised by David Beckham but adopted by trendy dykes of the 'naughties', including Alex Parks, winner of BBC TV's *Fame Academy* in 2003.

— LESBIAN MOVIES TO MAKE YOU SMILE —

If you're in need of a happy ending, these are the ones to watch:

All Over Me
Bound
Go Fish
Incredibly True Adventure of Two Girls In Love
But I'm A Cheerleader
Kissing Jessica Stein
Late Bloomers
Fire
It's In The Water
If These Walls Could Talk 2
Everything's Relative
When Night Is Falling

— A BRIEF BIO OF kd lang: THE BARE ESSENTIALS —

- Full name kathryn dawn lang.

- Born 2 November 1961 in Edmonton, Canada.

- Childhood spent in Consort, Alberta.

- Threw award-winning javelin in high school.

- Studied music at Red Deer College, dabbling in country and folk.

- Vegetarian and devout animal-lover.

- Won the Best Female Country Vocal Performance Grammy Award in 1989 for 'Full Moon Of Love', her first Top 25 hit.

- Publicly declared her lesbianism shortly after the release of her *Ingénue* album, thereafter ensuring a loyal following in the lesbian and gay community.

- Starred in the Percy Adlon film *Salmonberries* (1991), in which her butch ice-packing character falls in love with the visiting librarian.

— AUSTRALIAN CAMP —

Early Australian homosexual political organisations were pretty thin on the ground. The Daughters of Bilitis had a small chapter in Melbourne and is purported to be the first 'homophile' organisation down under, sometime during the 1970s. At around the same time, in July 1970, John Ware and Christabel Poll formed the first really mainstream gay-lib movement in Australia, calling themselves the Campaign Against Moral Persecution. This was, of course, abbreviated to CAMP, the usual Aussie term for 'homosexual'.

— LONGEST TV KISS BETWEEN TWO WOMEN —

In *Will And Grace*, episode 3 of season 5, Karen and Grace, the show's two lead female characters, kissed for a TV-record-breaking 14 seconds. During the marathon smooch, they re-enact a kiss that Grace had with her boyfriend Leo, so it can't be considered a strictly lesbian kiss. Nevertheless, Karen's bisexuality is a running gag, and in series 3 she even had a flashback to the relationship she'd had with Martina Navratilova, who made a guest appearance.

— GIRLS WRITING ABOUT BOYS —

Mary Renault was born in England in 1905 and was educated in Oxford. She trained to be a nurse just before World War II and wrote in her hours off throughout the conflict. After the war, she made South Africa her home and spent the rest of her life there, writing under the pseudonym Mary Challans. Some of her novels dealt with lesbianism but, perhaps more notably, some were specifically about male homosexuality. *The Last Of The Wine* and *The Charioteer* are two such cases, and the former has never been out of print, a testimony to its enduring popularity.

Mary lived with her presumed partner, Julie Mullard, for 50 years until her death in 1983. Her literature is often compared with that of Marguerite Yourcenar, who also wrote about male homosexuality.

— INDEX —